# The True Dawn
# An *Ahl as-Sunnah* Refutation of 'Salafī' Doctrine

# THE TRUE DAWN

## An *Ahl as-Sunnah* Refutation of 'Salafī' Doctrine

*by*

Shaykh Jamil Effendi al-Sidqi Al-Zahawi

Translated into English with Annotation and Notes by
Shaykh Muhammad Hisham Kabbani

Edited by Gibril Fouad al-Haddad

INSTITUTE FOR SPIRITUAL & CULTURAL UNDERSTANDING

First English translation published as: *The Doctrine of the Ahl al-Sunna Versus the "Salafī" Movement,* 1996 by Al-Sunna Foundation of America (USA) under ISBN: 1-871031-47-8

Publisher: Institute for Spiritual & Cultural Advancement
ISBN: 978-1-938058-73-8



Published in the US by
Institute for Spiritual & Cultural Advancement
17195 Silver Parkway #401,
Fenton, MI 48430 USA
Tel: (810) 593-2222
Email: sales@isn1.net
Purchase online at: http://www.isn1.net

Library of Congress Cataloging-in-Publication Data

Al-Zahawi, Jamil Effendi Sidqi (1863-1936)
[al-fajr al-sadiq fi al-radd `ala munkir al-*tawassul* wa al-khawariq. English]
The Doctrine of Ahl al-Sunna Versus the "Salafī" Movement / translated by Shaykh Muhammad Hisham Kabbani
p.120 cm.
Indices.
1. Islam--doctrines. 2. Heretics, Muslim. 3. Islamic sects.
4. Wahhābiyah. I. Kabbani, Shaykh Muḥammad Hisham.
II. Title
ISBN: 1-871031-47-8

بسم الله الرحمن الرحيم

وَصَلَّى ٱللَّهُ عَلَى سَيِّدِنَا مُحَمَّدٍ وَآلِهِ وَصَحْبِهِ وَسَلَّمَ

# THE DOCTRINE OF AHL AL-SUNNA VERSUS THE "SALAFĪ" MOVEMENT

﴿ وَقُلْ جَآءَ ٱلْحَقُّ وَزَهَقَ ٱلْبَـٰطِلُ ۚ إِنَّ ٱلْبَـٰطِلَ كَانَ زَهُوقًا ﴾

***And say: "Truth has come and falsehood has vanished away. Lo! falsehood is ever bound to vanish."*** [1]

[1] Sūrat al-Isrā [The Night Journey], 17:81.

# Prologue

Praise belongs to Allah Who has made truth clearly distinct from error, who puts down innovation and innovators and raises high the Sunna of the Prophet ﷺ, Peace be upon him, and the people who follow it. Praise belongs to Allah Who in every century inspires a group of scholarly people to defend the Way of the Prophet ﷺ, from the distortions of the ignorant—those who call the majority of Muslims *mushrik* (idolaters) and *mubtadi*ʿ (innovators) and *kāfir* (disbelievers), falsely claiming that they alone are saved. Salutations and greetings upon the Prophet ﷺ, his Family, and his Companions who are the exemplars and guardians of the Sunna.

# Contents

The Reason for This Book ........ 13

Publisher's Notes ........ 15

About the Book ........ 17

About the Author ........ 19

Ahl al-Sunna Condemnations of the Wahhabī/Salafī Heresies: A Select Bibliography ........ 23

Forty *Aḥādīth* on the Khawārij which the Scholars Consider to Apply to the Wahhābis ........ 33

The True Dawn: A Refutation of Those Who Deny the Validity of Using Means to Allah and the Miracles of Saints ........ 65

1: The Origin of the Wahhābi Sect ........ 65

2: The Wahhābis and their Recent Rebellion (1905) ........ 74

3: The Wahhābi Creed ........ 76

4: Their Making Allah Into A Body (*Tajsīm*) ........ 81

5: How the Wahhābis Cast Aside Reason ........ 86

6: Wahhābi Rejection of Consensus (*Ijma'*) ........ 89

7: The Wahhābis Denial of the Principle of Analogy (*Qiyās*) ........ 96

8: Their Denial of *Taqlīd* and of the *Ijtihād* of Past Sunni Scholars ........ 99

9: Their Naming Muslims Disbelievers (*Takfīr*) ........ 105

10: Apostasies and Heresies ........ 106

11: *Tawassul* (Using means): Evidence for its Permissibility 124

12: Wahhābis Claim: Anyone Visiting a Grave is a Disbeliever ........ 144

13: The Wahhābis' *takfīr* of the one who swears, makes a vow, or sacrifices by other than Allah ........................................ 158

Conclusion ........................................................................ 163

## The Reason for This Book

This brief but excellent book by the Iraqi scholar Al-Zahāwī (1863-1936) is published in English for the first time, by Allah's grace, to give our Muslim brother in the West the necessary historical background on important questions of belief and methodology which are currently under attack from certain quarters of our Community. It is a companion volume to our books entitled *Islamic Doctrine and Beliefs According to Ahl al-Sunna.*[2]

Islam, in our understanding and that of the majority of Muslims, both scholars and non-scholars, is the Islam of *Ahl al-Sunnah wa al-Jamā'ah*—The People of the Way of the Prophet ﷺ and the Community of Muslims. Chief and foremost among them are the true *Salaf* of Islam: the Companions, the Successors, and their Successors according to the Prophet's sound hadith in Muslim: "The best century is my century, then the one following it, then the one following that." All the scholars understood by that hadith that the true *Salaf* were the models of human behavior and correct belief for us Muslims and for all mankind, that to follow them was to follow the Prophet ﷺ, and that to follow the Prophet ﷺ was to achieve salvation according to Allah's order:

مَّن يُطِعِ ٱلرَّسُولَ فَقَدْ أَطَاعَ ٱللَّهَ

*Whoever obeys the Prophet obeys Allah;*[3]

In our time, however, the name *Salaf* has been usurped by a movement which seeks to impose its own narrow interpretation of Religion towards a re-fashioning of the teachings of Islam. The adherents of this movement call themselves "Salafī." Such an appellation is baseless since the true *Salaf* knew no such school as the "Salafī" school nor even called themselves by that

[2]Volumes 1 through 7, pub. As-Sunnah Foundation of America (1996).
[3] Sūratu 'n-Nisā [Women], 4:80.

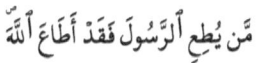

name; the only general name they recognized for themselves was that of Muslim. As an eminent scholar has stated, the Salafīyya is not a recognized school of thought in Islam, rather, it refers to a blessed historical period of our glorious past.

In reality, today's so-called "Salafī" movement, now about thirty years old, is the modern outgrowth of an two-century old heresy spawned by a scholar of the Najd area in the Eastern part of the Arabian peninsula by the name of Muḥammad ibn 'Abd al-Wahhāb (1703-1792). This scholar has been refuted by a long line of scholars both in his time and ours. Their names and the titles of some of their excellent refutations are found in the bibliography given at the end of this introduction.

In essence, Salafīsm and Wahhābism are the same, but the latter is identified by its founder while the former takes the name of the Salaf and makes it its own. Yet both Salafīsm and Wahhābism depart from the belief and practice of the Salaf, as the present book abundantly makes clear.

## Publisher's Notes

This book is specifically designed for readers relatively familiar with Islamic and Sufi terms. Qur'ānic quotes are centered, highlighted in bold and italics and footnoted, citing chapter name, number and verse.

### Universally Recognized Symbols

Muslims around the world typically offer praise upon speaking, hearing, or reading the name "*Allāh*" and any of the Islamic names of God. Muslims also offer salutation and/or invoke blessing upon speaking, hearing or reading the names of Prophet Muḥammad, other prophets, his family, his companions, and saints. We have applied the following international standards, using Arabic calligraphy and lettering:

ﷺ *ṣall-Allāhu ʿalayhi wa sallam* (God's blessings and greetings of peace be upon him) following the names of the Prophet ﷺ.

ﷷ *ʿalayhi 's-salām* (peace be upon him) following the names of other prophets, angels, and Khiḍr.

ﷷ *ʿalayhā 's-salām* (peace be upon her) following the name of Mary, Mother of Jesus.

ﷵ/ﷵ *raḍīy-Allāhu ʿanhu/ʿanhā* (may God be pleased with him/her) following the name of a male or female companion of the Prophet ﷺ.

ق *qaddas-Allāhu sirrah* (may God exalt his secret) following the name of a saint.

## Transliteration

Transliteration is provided to facilitate correct pronunciation and is based on the following system:

| Symbol | Trans-literation | Symbol | Trans-literation | Vowels: Long | |
|---|---|---|---|---|---|
| ء | ' | ط | ṭ | آ ى | ā |
| ب | b | ظ | ẓ | و | ū |
| ت | t | ع | ' | ي | ī |
| ث | th | غ | gh | Short | |
| ج | j | ف | f | ـَ | a |
| ح | ḥ | ق | q | ـُ | u |
| خ | kh | ك | k | ـِ | i |
| د | d | ل | l | | |
| ذ | dh | م | m | | |
| ر | r | ن | n | | |
| ز | z | ه | h | | |
| س | s | و | w | | |
| ش | sh | ي | y | | |
| ص | ṣ | ة | ah; at | | |
| ض | ḍ | ال | al-/'l- | | |

## About the Book

Al-Zahāwī displays a profound mastery of the proofs of Ahl al-Sunna which he presents in a clear and systematic style. The book is divided into concise sections tracing the origins of the Wahhābi/Salafī movement and the teachings that this movement promotes in isolation of the doctrine of the majority of Muslims. After a brief historical overview of the bloody origins of Wahhābism and the "Salafī" creed, the author turns to investigate the foundations of the shari'a which have been targeted by the Wahhābi/Salafī movement for revision, namely:

- the Wahhābi/Salafī tampering of the doctrine of the pious Salaf concerning Allah's essence and attributes, and his freedom from body, size, or direction;
- their rejection of *ijma'* (scholarly consensus) and *qiyās* (analogy);
- their rejection of the sources and methodological foundations of *Ijtihād* (deriving qualified judgment) and *taqlīd* (following qualified judgment).
- The author then narrows down on the Wahhābi/Salafī practice of *takfīr*, which is their declaring Muslims unbelievers, according to criteria not followed by the pious Salaf but devised by modern-day "Salafīs."
- The author shows that the "Salafīs" went out of bounds in condemning the Umma (Muslim Community) on the question of *taqlīd*, declaring unbelievers all those who practice *taqlīd*, that is, the majority of Muslims.
- Finally, the author turns to the linchpin of "Salafī" philosophy: leaving the *ijmā'* of the true *Salaf* in declaring unbelievers all Muslims who use the Prophet Muḥammad's ﷺ intercession as a *wasīlah* or means of blessing.

## About the Author

Al-Shaykh Jamīl Effendī al-Ṣidqī Al-Zahāwī was the son of the Mufti of Iraq and a descendant of Khalid ibn al-Walid ﷺ. He was educated in the Islamic sciences chiefly by his father and, besides going on to become the greatest Arabic and Persian poet of modern Iraq, was also a literary master in the other two Islamic languages of the time: Turkish and Kurdish.

Al-Zahāwī gave early proofs of his scholarly talents. By the age of forty he had served on the board of education in Baghdad, as the director of the state printing office, as editor of the chief state publication, al-Zawrā', and as a member of the Baghdad court of appeal. The second half of his life was devoted to writing, journalism, and teaching. He taught philosophy and Arabic literature in Istanbul and law in Baghdad. A prolific writer, at one point he declined the office of court poet and historian of Iraq offered him by King Fayṣal. In addition to the above he was scientifically inclined and wrote papers on various scientific topics such as electricity and the power of repulsion, all this despite a chronic disease of the spine which had crippled him from his twenty-fifth year.

At the turn of the century Arabia had witnessed the return of the Wahhābis to power and the open rebellion of their forces against the Caliph of the Islamic community. What was worse, the Wahhābi heresy was knocking at the gates of Baghdad, and the scholars of Ahl al-Sunna spoke out in order to stem its rising tide. In 1905 at the age of 42 and upon the request of his father Al-Zahāwī published this eloquent indictment of the sect's innovations in doctrine and jurisprudence, refuting its tenets one by one. He named the book, of which the present work forms the major part, *al-Fajr al-ṣādiq fī al-radd ʿalā munkirī al-tawassul wa al-khawāriq* ("The True Dawn: A Refutation of Those Who Deny The Validity of Using Means to Allah and the Miracles of Saints"). The title indicates Zahāwī's opinion, reminiscent of that of other scholars who wrote similar refutations, that the Wahhābi position on *tawassul* represents the essence of their deviation from the beliefs of Ahl al-Sunna, although it is but one of their many divergences with Sunni Muslims.

Zahāwī's brilliant style, his acute sense of balance and moderation, and his luminous logic and concision gave this brief book an undisputed place of honor among modern works of heresiology. May Allah reward him with His generosity, as well as those who collaborated on this timely and all-beneficial translation for the edification of English-speaking Muslims. We warmly recommend this book to all the sincere students and teachers who are interested in the growth and dissemination of sound Islamic belief in the West.

مُبَارَكُ مَوْلَى إِبْرَاهِيمَ ابْنِ هِشَامٍ الْمَرَابِطِيُّ قَالَ: ثَضَا الْعَطَّافِ بْنِ خَالِدٍ، عَنْ نَافِعٍ، عَنْ ابْنِ عُمَرَ مَرْفُوعًا، بِاللَّفْظِ: «يَا ابْنَ عُمَرَ، دِينَكَ دِينَكَ، إِنَّمَا هُوَ لَحْمُكَ وَدَمُكَ، فَانْظُرْ عَمَّنْ تَأْخُذْ، خُذْ عَنِ الَّذِينَ اسْتَقَامُوا، وَلَا تَأْخُذْ عَنِ الَّذِينَ مَالُوا».

The Prophet of Allah ﷺ said to Ibn ʿUmar ؓ, "O Ibn ʿUmar! This Religion is our flesh and our blood, so watch from whom you take it"[4]: in our time it is a duty to inform ourselves as to the soundness of the religious teaching which we are receiving and passing on to our children. For our own sake and theirs, we must discern the sources of such teaching with extreme caution, sifting the sound from the unsound, correcting what is wrong with our hand, our tongue, and our heart.

Muslims of the twenty-first century should beware of the renewed onslaught on their beliefs being conducted today from within our Communities East and West. In the name of Qur'an and Sunna, but actually supported by certain regimes pursuing specific ideologies, "Salafīs" are taking over the mosques built

[4] Al-Khaṭīb al-Baghdādī. This hadith was considered weak. A similar wording though, is related in *Ṣaḥīḥ Muslim* as a statement of Muḥammad ibn Sīrīn (a *tabīʿī*) with an authentic chain. The remaining portion of the hadith translates: "Take from those who are upright, and do not take from those who have deviated."

by Ahl al-Sunna in Europe and North America—mostly Indian and Pakistani immigrants—by means of elections and fundings. It is the duty of all Muslims to ascertain that the mosques of Allah continue as centers of sound Islamic practice, not "Salafī" practice. This can only be done if one first appraises oneself of the reality of "Salafī" beliefs which are different from those of the main body of Muslims.

وَعَنْ عَبْدِ اللَّهِ بْنِ عَمْرٍو قَالَ قَالَ رَسُولُ اللَّهِ ﷺ: «لَيَأْتِيَنَّ عَلَى أُمَّتِى مَا أَتَى عَلَى بَنِى إِسْرَائِيلَ حَذْوَ النَّعْلِ بِالنَّعْلِ حَتَّى إِنَّ كَانَ مِنْهُمْ مَنْ أَتَى أُمَّهُ عَلَانِيَةً لَكَانَ فِى أُمَّتِى مَنْ يَصْنَعُ ذَلِكَ وَإِنَّ بَنِى إِسْرَائِيلَ تَفَرَّقَتْ عَلَى ثِنْتَيْنِ وَسَبْعِينَ مِلَّةً وَتَفْتَرِقُ أُمَّتِى عَلَى ثَلَاثٍ وَسَبْعِينَ مِلَّةً كُلُّهُمْ فِى النَّارِ إِلَّا مِلَّةً وَاحِدَةً قَالُوا وَمَن هِىَ يَا رَسُولَ اللَّهِ قَالَ مَا أَنَا عَلَيْهِ وأصحابى» . رَوَاهُ التِّرْمِذِىّ

The Prophet ﷺ said: "My Community will split into seventy-three sects. All of them will be in the fire except one group." They asked: "Who are they, O Messenger of Allah?" He said: "Those that follow my way and that of my companions."[5]

This is a rallying-cry to the Firm Rope of 1,418 years of mainstream Islam and an invitation to reject the absurd claim of the "Salafī" movement that it is they, and not Ahl al-Sunna, who are the Saved Group. As Zahāwī—may Allah have mercy on him—asks: If the saved group are those who came after Muḥammad ibn ʿAbd al-Wahhāb, then what is the status of all those who came before him, and that of the majority of those who came after him—that is, *Ahl al-Sunnah wa al-Jamāʿah*?

This warning is not meant as an attack on Islamic unity. On the contrary, our cry of alarm must be understood as a reaffirmation that the Saved Group which the Prophet ﷺ mentioned in his

---

[5]A sound (*ṣaḥīḥ*) ḥadīth related by al-Tirmidhī, Abū Dāwūd, and al-Dārimī.

hadith are the People of the Way of the Prophet ﷺ and their scholars. Those scholars have spoken in no uncertain terms in condemnation of the innovations of Wahhābis and "Salafīs" in our time, as the present book and the bibliography below, *al-ḥamdu li-llāh*, prove beyond doubt.

May Allah give victory to those who stand truly for the way of His Prophet, Blessings and Peace be upon him. O Believers, read this book and take heed of its message. We conclude this brief introduction with a selective list of authors and works of Ahl al-Sunna scholars in whose pages the deviations of Wahhābis and Salafīs are exposed time after time and conclusively refuted. We look forward to their translations and recommend every one of them. And all praise belongs to Allah, the Lord of the Worlds.

Shaykh Muhammad Hisham Kabbani
Los Altos, California
1 Muharram 1418
19 May 1996

# *AHL AL-SUNNA* CONDEMNATIONS OF THE WAHHĀBI/SALAFĪ HERESIES: A SELECT BIBLIOGRAPHY

**Al-Aḥsāʾī** al-Miṣrī, Aḥmad **(1753–1826):** Unpublished manuscript of a refutation of the Wahhābi sect. His son Shaykh Muḥammad ibn Aḥmad ibn ʿAbd al-Laṭīf al-Aḥsāʾī also wrote a book refuting them.

**Al-Aḥsāʾī**, al-Sayyid ʿAbd al-Raḥmān: wrote a sixty-seven verse poem which begins with the verse:

> *Badat fitnatun kal-layli qad ghaṭṭat al-āfāqa wa shāʿat fa kādat tuballigh al-gharb wa al-sharq*
> [A confusion came about like nightfall covering the skies and became widespread almost reaching the whole world]

**Al-ʿAmrāwī,** ʿAbd al-Ḥayy, and ʿAbd al-Ḥakīm Murād (Jāmiʿat al-Qarawiyyīn, al-Maghrib): *al-Taḥdhīr min al-Ightirār bimā Jāʾa fī Kitāb al-Ḥiwār* [Fās: Jāmiʿat al-Qarawiyyīn, 1984]ʿAta' Allah al-Makki: *al-Ṣārim al-Hindī fī al-ʿUnūq al-Najdī* ["The Indian Scimitar on the Najdī's Neck"].

**Al-Azharī,** ʿAbd Rabbih ibn Sulaymān al-Shāfiʿī (The author of *Sharḥ Jāmiʿ al-Uṣūl li-aḥādīth al-Rasūl*, a foundational work in *Uṣūl al-Fiqh*: *Fayḍ al-Wahhāb fī Bayān Ahl al-Ḥaqq wa man ḍalla ʿan al-ṣawāb*) 4 vols. ["Allah's Outpouring in Differentiating the True Muslims From Those Who Deviated from the Truth"].

**Al-ʿAẓẓamī**, ʿAllāma al-Shaykh Salāma (d. 1379H): *al-Barāhīn al-Sāṭiʿah* ["The Radiant Proofs..."].

**Al-Barakāt** al-Shāfiʿī al-Aḥmadī al-Makkī, ʿAbd al-Wahhāb ibn Aḥmad: unpublished manuscript of a refutation of the Wahhābi sect.

**al-Bulāqī,** Muṣṭafá al-Miṣrī wrote a refutation to Sanʿa'i's poem in which the latter had praised Ibn ʿAbd al-Wahhāb. It is in

Samnūdī's *Sa'adat al-Dārayn* and consists in 126 verses beginning thus:

*Bi-ḥamdi waliyyi al-ḥamdi lā al-dhammi astabdi*
*Wa bi-l-ḥaqqi lā bi-l-khalqi li-l-ḥaqqi astahdi*
[By the glory of the Owner of glory, not baseness, do I overcome;
And by Allah, not by creatures, do I seek guidance to Allah]

**Al-Būṭī,** Muḥammad Sa'īd Ramaḍān (University of Damascus): *Al-Salafīyyatu marḥalatun zamāniyyatun mubārakatun lā madhhabun islāmī,* ["The Salafīyya is a blessed historical period not an Islamic school of law"] (Damascus: Dar al-fikr, 1988); *Al-Lāmadhhabiyyah akhṭaru bida'atin tuhaddidu al-sharī'ata al-islāmiyyah* ["Non-madhhabism is the most dangerous innovation presently menacing Islamic law"] (Damascus: Maktabat al-Farabi, n.d.).

**Al-Dāhish** ibn 'Abd Allāh, Dr. (Jāmi'at al-'Arabiyyah bi-l-Maghrib), ed. *Munāẓarah 'Ilmiyyah bayna 'Alī ibn Muḥammad al-Sharīf wa al-Imām Aḥmad ibn Idrīs fī al-Radd 'alā Wahhābiyyat Najd, Tihāmah, wa 'Asīr* ["Scholarly Debate Between the Sharif and Aḥmad ibn Idris Against the Wahhābis of Najd, Tihāmah, and 'Asīr"].

**Dahlān**, Al-Sayyid Aḥmad ibn Zaynī (d. 1304/1886). Mufti of Mecca and Shaykh al-Islam (highest religious authority in the Ottoman jurisdiction) for the Hijaz region: *al-Durar al-saniyyah fī al-Radd 'alā al-Wahhābiyyah* ["The Pure Pearls in Answering the Wahhābis"] pub. Egypt 1319 & 1347 H; *Fitnat al-Wahhābiyyah* ["The Wahhābi Fitna"]; *Khulāṣat al-Kalām fī Bayān Umarā' al-Balad al-Ḥarām* ["The Summation Concerning the Leaders of the Sacrosanct Country"], a history of the Wahhābi *fitna* in Najd and the Hijaz.

**Al-Dajwī,** Ḥamd Allāh: al-Baṣā'ir li-Munkirī al-Tawassul ka-Amthāl Muḥammad ibn 'Abd al-Wahhāb ["The Evident Proofs

Against Those Who Deny the Seeking of Intercession Like Muḥammad Ibn ʿAbdul Wahhāb"].

**Al-Baghdādī** al-Ḥanafī, Shaykh al-Islām Dāwūd ibn Sulaymān (1815–1881 CE): *al-Minḥah al-Wahbiyyah fī Radd al-Wahhābiyyah* ["The Divine Dispensation Concerning the Wahhābi Deviation"]; *Ashadd al-Jihād fī Ibṭāl Daʿwā al-Ijtihād* ["The Most Violent Jihad in Proving False Those Who Falsely Claim *Ijtihād*"].

**Al-Fulānī** al-Maghribī, al-Muḥaddith Ṣāliḥ: authored a large volume collating the answers of scholars of the Four Schools to Muḥammad ibn ʿAbd al-Wahhāb.

**Al-Ḥabībī**, Muḥammad ʿĀshiq al-Raḥmān: *ʿAdhāb Allāh al-Mujdī li-Junūn al-Munkir al-Najdī* ["Allah's Terrible Punishment for the Mad Rejector From Najd"].

**Al-Ḥaddād**, al-Sayyid al-ʿAlawī ibn Aḥmad ibn Ḥasan ibn al-Qutb Sayyidī ʿAbd Allāh ibn ʿAlawī al-Ḥaddād al-Shāfiʿī: *al-Sayf al-Bāṭir li-ʿUnuq al-Munkir ʿalā al-Akābir* ["The Sharp Sword for the Neck of the Assailant of Great Scholars"]. Unpublished manuscript of about 100 folios; *Miṣbāḥ al-Anām wa-Jalāʾ al-Ẓalām fī Radd Shubah al-Bidʿī al-Najdī allatī Aḍalla bihā al-ʿAwāmm* ["The Lamp of Mankind and the Illumination of Darkness Concerning the Refutation of the Errors of the Innovator From Najd by Which He Had Misled the Common People"]. Published 1325H.

**Al-Ḥamāmī** al-Miṣrī, Shaykh Muṣṭafā: *Ghawth al-ʿIbād bi-Bayān al-Rashād* ["The Helper of Allah's Servants According to the Affirmation of Guidance"].

**Al-Ḥilmī** al-Qādirī al-Iskandarī, Shaykh Ibrāhīm: *Jalāl al-Ḥaqq fī Kashf Aḥwāl Ashrār al-Khalq* ["The Splendor of Truth in Exposing the Worst of People] (pub. 1355H).

**Al-Ḥusaynī,** ʿĀmilī Muḥsin (1865–1952): *Kashf al-Irtiyāb fī Atbāʿ Muḥammad ibn ʿAbd al-Wahhāb* ["The Dispelling of

Doubt Concerning the Followers of Muḥammad ibn ʻAbd al-Wahhāb”]. [Beirut]: Dar al-Taʻaruf li-l-Maṭbuʻat, ?

**Ibn ʻAbd al-Laṭīf** al-Shāfiʻī, ʻAbd Allāh: *Tajrīd Sayf al-Jihād ʻalā Muddaʻī al-Ijtihād* [“The drawing of the sword of jihad against the false claimants to *Ijtihād*”].

The family of Ibn ʻAbd al-Razzāq al-Ḥanbalī in Zubara and Bahrayn possess both manuscript and printed refutations by scholars of the Four Schools from Mecca, Madina, al-Ahsa', al-Basra, Baghdad, Aleppo, Yemen and other Islamic regions.

**ibn ʻAbd al-Wahhāb** al-Najdī, al-ʻAllāmah al-Shaykh Sulaymān: *al-Ṣawāʻiq al-Ilāhiyyah fī al-Radd ʻalā al-Wahhābiyyah* [“Divine Lightnings in Answering the Wahhābis”]. Ed. Ibrāhīm Muḥammad al-Baṭāwī. Cairo: Dar al-insan, 1987. Offset reprint by Waqf Ikhlas, Istanbul: Hakikat Kitabevi, 1994. Prefaces by Shaykh Muḥammad ibn Sulaymān al-Kurdī al-Shāfiʻī and Shaykh Muḥammad Ḥayyān al-Sindī (Muḥammad ibn ʻAbd al-Wahhāb's shaykh) to the effect that Ibn ʻAbd al-Wahhāb is *ḍāll muḍill* (“misguided and misguiding”).

**Ibn ʻĀbidīn** al-Ḥanafī, al-Sayyid Muḥammad Amīn: *Radd al-Muḥtār ʻalā al-Durr al-Mukhtār,* Vol. 3, Kitab al-Īmān, Bab al-bughat [“Answer to the Perplexed: A Commentary on “The Chosen Pearl,” Book of Belief, Chapter on Rebels]. Cairo: Dar al-Tibaʻa al-Misriyya, 1272 H.

**Ibn ʻAfāliq** al-Ḥanbalī, Muḥammad ibn ʻAbd al-Raḥmān: *Taḥakkum al-Muqallidīn bi-Man Iddaʻā Tajdīd al-Dīn* [Sarcasm of the *muqallids* against the false claimants to the Renewal of Religion]. A very comprehensive book refuting the Wahhābi heresy and posting questions which Ibn ʻAbdul Wahhāb and his followers were unable to answer for the most part.

**Ibn Dāwūd** al-Ḥanbalī, ʻAfīf al-Dīn ʻAbd Allāh: *al-Ṣawāʻiq wa al-Ruʻūd* [“Lightnings and thunder”], a very important book in 20 chapters. According to the Mufti of Yemen Shaykh al-ʻAlawī ibn Aḥmad al-Ḥaddād, the mufti of Yemen, “This book has received the approval of the '*'Ulamā'* of Basra, Baghdad, Aleppo, and Ahsa' [Arabian peninsula]. It was summarized by Muḥammad ibn Bashir the qadi of Ra's al-Khayma in Oman."

**Ibn Ghalbūn** al-Lībī also wrote a refutation in forty verses of al-San'ani's poem in which the latter had praised Ibn 'Abd al-Wahhāb. It is in Samnudi's *Sa'ādat al-Dārayn* and begins thus:

*Salāmī 'alā ahl al-ṣabāti wa al-rushdī*
*wa laysa 'alā Najdī wa man ḥalla fī Najdī*
[My salutation is upon the people of truth and guidance
And not upon Najd nor the one who settled in Najd]

**Ibn Khalīfah** 'Ulyāwī al-Azharī: *Hādhihi 'Aqīdat al-Salaf wa al-Khalaf fī Dhāt Allāh Ta'ālā wa Ṣifātihi wa Af'ālihi wa al-Jawāb al-Ṣaḥīḥ li-mā Waqa'a fīhi al-Khilāf min al-Furū' bayna al-Dā'īn li al-Salafiyyah wa Atbā' al-Madhāhib al-Arba'ah al-Islāmiyyah* ["This is the doctrine of the Predecessors and the Descendants concerning the divergences in the branches between those who call to *al-Salafiyya* and the followers of the Four Islamic Schools of Law"] (Damascus: Matba'at Zayd ibn Thabit, 1398/1977.

**al-Kawtharī** al-Ḥanafī, Muḥammad Zāhid: *Maqālāt al-Kawtharī.* (Cairo: al-Maktabah al-Azhariyah li al-Turath, 1994).

**al-Kawwāsh** al-Tūnisī, al-'Allāmah al-Shaykh Ṣāliḥ: his refutation of the Wahhābi sect is contained in Ibrāhīm ibn 'Uthmān al-Samannūdī's: *Sa'ādat al-Dārayn fī al-Radd 'alā al-Firqatayn.*

**Khazbak,** Shaykh Ḥasan: *al-Maqālāt al-Wāfiyyāt fī al-Radd 'alā al-Wahhābiyyah* ["Complete Treatise in Refuting the Wahhābis"].

**Makhlūf,** Muḥammad Ḥasanayn: *Risālah fī Ḥukm al-Tawassul bi-l-Anbiyā' wa-l-Awliyā'* ["Treatise on the Ruling Concerning the Use of Prophets and Saints as Intermediaries"].

**al-Mālikī**, al-Muḥaddith Muḥammad al-Ḥasan ibn 'Alawī al-Ḥusaynī: *Mafāhīm Yajibu an Tuṣaḥḥaḥ* ["Notions that should be corrected"] 4th ed. (Dubai: Hashr ibn Muḥammad Dalmuk,

1986); *Muḥammad al-Insān al-Kāmil* ["Muḥammad, the Perfect Human Being"] 3rd ed. (Jeddah: Dar al-Shuruq, 1404/1984).

**Al-Mashrifī** al-Mālikī al-Jazāʾirī: *Iẓhār al-ʿUqūq mimman Manaʿa al-Tawassul bi-l-Nabī wa al-Walī al-Ṣadūq* ["The Exposure of the Disobedience of Those Who Forbid Using the Intermediary of the Prophets and the Truthful Saints].

**Al-Mirghānī** al-Ṭāʾifī, al-ʿAllāmah ʿAbd Allāh ibn Ibrāhīm (d. 1793): *Taḥrīḍ al-Aghbiyāʾ ʿalā al-Istighāthah bi-l-Anbiyāʾ wa-l-Awliyāʾ* ["The Provocations of the Ignorant Against Seeking the Help of Prophets and Saints"] (Cairo: al-Halabi, 1939).

**Muʿīn al-Ḥaqq** al-Dihlawī (d. 1289 AH): *Sayf al-Jabbār al-Maslūl ʿalā Aʿdāʾ al-Abrār* ["The Sword of the Almighty Drawn Against the Enemies of the Pure Ones"].

**Al-Muwaysī** al-Yamanī, ʿAbd Allāh ibn ʿĪsā Unpublished manuscript of a refutation of the Wahhābi sect.

**Al-Nabhānī** al-Shāfiʿī, al-Qāḍī al-Muḥaddith Yūsuf ibn Ismāʿīl (1850–1932): *Shawāhid al-Ḥaqq fī al-Istighāthah bi-Sayyid al-Khalq* ﷺ ["The Proofs of Truth in the Seeking of the Intercession of the Prophet ﷺ"].

**Al-Qabbānī** al-Baṣrī al-Shāfiʿī, al-ʿAllāmah Aḥmad ibn ʿAlī: A manuscript treatise in approximately 10 chapters.

**Al-Qādumī** al-Nābulusī al-Ḥanbalī, ʿAbd Allāh: *Riḥlah* ("Journey")

**Al-Qazwīnī,** Muḥammad Ḥasan (d. 1825): *al-Barāhīn al-Jaliyyah fī Dafʿ Tashkīkāt al-Wahhābiyyah* ["The Plain Demonstrations That Dispel the Aspersions of the Wahhābis"]. Ed. Muḥammad Munir al-Husayni al-Milani. 1st ed. Beirut: Mu'assasat al-Wafa', 1987.

**Al-Qudsī:** *al-Suyūf al-Ṣiqāl fī Aʿnāq man Ankara ʿalā al-Awliyāʾ baʿd al-Intiqāl* ["The Burnished Swords on the Necks of Those Who Deny the Role of Saints After Their Leaving This World"].

**Al-Rifā'ī,** Yūsuf al-Sayyid Hāshim, President of the World Union of Islamic Propagation and Information: *Adillāt Ahl al-Sunnah wa al-Jamā'ah aw al-Radd al-Muḥkam al-Manī' 'alā Munkarāt wa Shubuhāt Ibn Manī' fī Tahajjumi-hi 'alā al-Sayyid Muḥammad 'Alawī al-Mālikī al-Makkī* ["The Proofs of the People of the Way of the Prophet ﷺ and the Muslim Community: or, the Strong and Decisive Refutation of Ibn Mani''s Aberrations and Aspersions in his Assault on Muḥammad 'Alawi al-Maliki al-Makki"] (Kuwait: Dar al-siyasa, 1984).

**Al-Samannūdī** al-Manṣūrī, al-'Allāmah al-Shaykh Ibrāhīm: *Sa'ādat al-Dārayn fī al-Radd 'alā al-Firqatayn al-Wahhābiyyah wa Muqallidat al-Ẓāhiriyyah* ["Bliss in the Two Abodes: Refutation of the Two Sects, Wahhābis and Ẓāhiri Followers"].

**Al-Saqqāf** al-Shāfi'ī, Ḥasan ibn 'Alī, Islamic Research Institute, Amman, Jordan: *al-Ighāthah bi-Adillāt al-Istighāthah wa al-Radd al-Mubīn 'alā Munkirī al-Tawassul* ["The Mercy of Allah in the Proofs of Seeking Intercession and the Clear Answer to Those who Reject it"]; *Ilqām al-Ḥajar li al-Mutatāwil 'alā al-Ashā'irah min al-Bashar* ["The Stoning of All Those Who Attack Ash'aris"]; *Qāmūs Shaṭā'im al-Albānī wa al-Alfāẓ al-Munkarah allatī Yaṭluquhā fī Ḥaqq 'Ulamā' al-Ummah wa Fuḍalā'ihā wa Ghayrihim...* ["Encyclopedia of al-Albani's Abhorrent Expressions Which He Uses Against the Scholars of the Community, its Eminent Men, and Others..."] Amman : Dar al-Imam al-Nawawī, 1993.

**Al-Ṣāwī** al-Miṣrī, Aḥmad ibn Muḥammad: *Ḥāshiyat al-Ṣāwī 'alā Tafsīr al-Jalālayn* ["Commentary on the Tafsir of the Two Jalal al-Din"].

**Sayf al-Dīn**, Aḥmad ibn Muḥammad: *Al-Albani Unveiled: An Exposition of His Errors and Other Important Issues*, 2nd ed. (London: s.n., 1994).

**al-Shattī** al-Atharī al-Ḥanbalī, al-Sayyid Muṣṭafā ibn Aḥmad ibn Ḥasan, Mufti of Syria: *al-Nuqūl al-Shar'iyyah fī al-Radd 'alā al-Wahhābiyyah* ["The Legal Proofs in Answering the Wahhābis"].

**al-Subkī,** al-Ḥāfiẓ Taqī al-Dīn (d. 756/1355): *al-Durra al-Muḍiyyah fī al-Radd 'alā Ibn Taymiyya*, ed. Muḥammad Zāhid al-Kawtharī ["The Luminous Pearl: A Refutation of Ibn Taymiyya"]; *al-Rasā'il al-Subkiyyah fī al-Radd 'alā Ibn Taymiyyah wa Tilmīdhihi Ibn Qayyim al-Jawziyyah,* ed. Kamāl al-Ḥūt (Beirut: 'Ālam al-Kutub, 1983) ["Subki's Treatises in Answer to Ibn Taymiyya and His Pupil Ibn Qayyim al-Jawziyya"]; *al-Sayf al-Saqīl fī al-Radd 'alā Ibn Zāfil,* (*Cairo:* Maṭba'at al-Sa'ādah, 1937) ["The Burnished Sword in Refuting Ibn Zafil (i.e., Ibn Qayyim al-Jawziyya)"] Cairo: Matba'at al-Sa'ada, 1937; *Shifā' al-Siqām fī Ziyārat Khayr al-Anām* ["The healing of the sick in visiting the Best of Creation"].

**Sunbūl** al-Ḥanafī al-Ṭā'ifī, 'Allāma Ṭāhir: *Sīmā al-Intiṣār li-l-Awliyā' al-Abrār* ["The Mark of Victory Belongs to Allah's Pure Friends"].

**Al-Ṭabāṭabā'ī** al-Baṣrī, al-Sayyid: also wrote a reply to San'ā'ī's poem, which was excerpted in Samnūdī's *Sa'ādat al-Dārayn.* After reading it, San'ā'ī reversed his position and said: "I have repented from what I said concerning the Najdī."

**Al-Tamīmī** al-Mālikī, 'Allāma Ismā'īl (d. 1248), Shaykh al-Islam in Tunis: wrote a refutation of a treatise of Ibn 'Abd al-Wahhāb.

**Al-Wazzānī,** al-Shaykh al-Mahdī, Mufti of Fes, Morocco: Wrote a refutation of Muḥammad 'Abduh's prohibition of *tawassul.*

**Al-Zahāwī** al-Baghdādī, Jamīl Effendī Ṣidqī (d. 1355/1936): *al-Fajr al-Ṣādiq fī al-Radd 'alā Munkirī al-Tawassul wa al-Khawāriq* ["The True Dawn in Refuting Those Who Deny the Seeking of Intercession and the Miracles of Saints"] Pub. 1323/1905 in Egypt.

**Al-Zamzamī** al-Shāfi'ī, Muḥammad Ṣāliḥ, Imām of the Maqām Ibrāhīm in Makkah, wrote a book in 20 chapters against them, according to al-Sayyid al-Ḥaddād.

**Aḥmad**, Qeyamuddin. *The Wahhābi movement in India.* 2nd rev. ed. New Delhi : Manohar, 1994.

# FORTY *AḤĀDĪTH* ON THE KHAWĀRIJ WHICH THE SCHOLARS CONSIDER TO APPLY TO THE WAHHĀBIS

For the most part these *aḥādīth* are cited in the Six Books of authentic traditions. They have been collated for the most part from the following two books written in refutation of the Wahhābi heresy:

a) al-Sayyid al-ʿAlawī ibn Aḥmad ibn Ḥasan ibn ʿAbd Allāh ibn ʿAlawī al-Ḥaddād: *Miṣbāḥ al-Anām wa Jalāʾ al-Ẓalām fī Radd Shubah al-Bidʿī al-Najdī allatī Adalla bihā al-ʿAwāmm* ["The Lamp of Creatures and the Illumination of Darkness Concerning the Refutation of the Errors of the Innovator From Najd by Which He Had Misled the Common People"] published 1325H.

b) al-Sayyid Aḥmad ibn Zaynī al-Dahlān (d. 1304/1886), Muftī of Makkah and Shaykh al-Islām in the Ḥijāz region of the Ottoman state: *Khulāṣat al-Kalām fī Bayān Umarāʾ al-Balad al-Ḥarām* ["The Summation Concerning the Leaders of the Holy Sanctuary"] (A History of the Wahhābi *Fitna* in Najd and the Hijaz) p. 234-236.

1.

عَنْ عَبْدِ اللَّهِ بْنِ عُمَرَ رَضِيَ اللَّهُ تَعَالَى عَنْهُمَا فِى وَصْفِ الْخَوَارِجِ «أنهم انْطَلَقوا إِلَى آياتٍ نَزَلَتْ فِى الكُفَّارِ، فجَعَلوها عَلَى المُؤْمنينَ»

Ibn Umar ☙ said in describing the Khawārij[6], "They transferred the Qur'anic verses meant to refer to unbelievers and made them refer to believers."[7]

---

[6] Khawārij = those outside.
[7] cited by al-Bukhārī without *isnad*, *Musnad* al-Imām Aḥmad, *al-Muṣannaf* of ʿAbd al-Razzāq, *Fatḥ al-Bārī* by Ibn Ḥajar traces it with a *ṣaḥīḥ* chain.

2.

عَنْ ابْنِ عُمَرَ رَضِى الله عَنْهُما أَنَّهُ ﷺ قَالَ: «أَخْوَفَ مَا أَخَافُ عَلَى أُمَّتِى رَجُلٌ مُتَأَوِّل لِلْقُرْآن يَضَعُهُ فِى غَيْرِ مَوْضِعِهِ»

The Prophet ﷺ said, "What I most fear in my community is a man who interprets verses of the Qur'an out of context."

3.

عَنْ سَالِمِ بْنِ عَبْدِ اللَّهِ، أَنَّ عَبْدَ اللَّهِ بْنَ عُمَرَ - رَضِى الله عَنْهُما - قَالَ سَمِعْتُ رَسُولَ اللَّهِ ﷺ يَقُولُ وَهْوَ عَلَى الْمِنْبَرِ «أَلاَ إِنَّ الْفِتْنَةَ هَا هُنَا - يُشِيرُ إِلَى الْمَشْرِقِ - مِنْ حَيْثُ يَطْلُعُ قَرْنُ الشَّيْطَانِ»

The Prophet ﷺ said, "The confusion [*fitna*] comes from there (and he pointed to the East)[8] whence the side of the head of Satan comes out."[9]

4.

عَنْ أَبِى سَعِيدٍ الخُدْرِىُّ ؓ عَنْ النَّبِيِّ ﷺ قَالَ: «يَخْرُجُ نَاسٌ مِنْ قِبَلِ المَشْرِقِ وَيَقْرَؤُونَ القُرْآنَ لَا يُجَاوِزُ تَرَاقِيَهُمْ يَمْرُقُونَ مُنَالِدَيْنِ كَمَا يَمْرُقُ السَّهْمُ مِنْ الرَّمْيَةِ ثُمَّ لَا يَعُودُونَ فِيهِ حَتَّى يَعُودَ السَّهْمُ إِلَى فَوْقِهَ» قِيلَ «مَا سِيمَاهُمْ » قَالَ سِيمَاهُمْ التَّحْلِيقُ أَوْ قَالَ «التَّسْبِيدَ»

The Prophet ﷺ said, "A people will come out from the East that recite Qur'an, but it will not go past their throats. They will pass through the religion (of Islam) like the arrow passes through its quarry. They will no more come back to the religion than the

---

[8] East = Najd in present-day Eastern Saudi Arabia.
[9] Bukhārī.

arrow will come back to its course. Their sign is that they shave (their heads)."[10]

5.

عَنْ أَنَسِ بْنِ مَالِكٍ ﷺ أَنَّ رَسُولَ اللَّهِ ﷺ قَالَ : « سَيَكُونُ فِى أُمَّتِى اخْتِلَافٌ وَ فِرْقَةُ قَوْمٍ يُحْسِنُونَ الْقِيْلَ وَ يُسِيئُونَ الْفِعْلَ وَ يَقْرَؤُونَ الْقُرْآنَ لَا يُجَاوِزُ تَرَاقِيَهُمْ يَحْقِرُ أَحَدُكُمْ صَلَاتَهُ مَعَ صَلَاتِهِمْ وَ صِيَامَهُ مَعَ صِيَامِهِمْ يَمْرُقُونَ مِنَ الدِّيْنِ مُرُوقَ السَّهْمِ مِنَ الرَّمِيَّةِ لَا يَرْجِعُ حَتَّى يُرَدَّ السَّهْمُ عَلَى فَوْقِهِ وَ هُمْ شِرَارُ الْخَلْقِ وَ الْخَلِيقَةُ طُوبَى لِمَنْ قَتَلَهُمْ وَ قَتَلُوهُ يَدْعُونَ إِلَى كِتَابِ اللَّهِ وَ لَيْسُوا مِنْهُ فِى شَىْءٍ مِنْ قَاتَلَهم كَانَ أَوْلَى بِاللَّهِ مِنْهُمْ » . قَالُوا: «يَا رَسُولَ اللَّهِ مَا سِيمَاهُمْ؟» قَالَ: «التَّحْلِيقُ»

The Prophet ﷺ said, "There will be in my Community a dissent and a faction, a people with excellent words and vile deeds. They will read Qur'an, but their faith does not go past their throats. They will pass through religion the way an arrow passes through its quarry. They will no more come back to the religion than the arrow will come back to its original course. They are the worst of human beings and the worst of all creation. The one who kills them or is killed by them is blessed. They summon to the Book of Allah but they have nothing to do with it. Whoever kills them is closer to Allah than they. Their sign is that they shave (their heads)."[11]

---

[10] Bukhārī, al-Nasāʾī, al-Bazzār.
[11] Al-Ḥākim al-Nīsābūrī in his *al-Mustadrak*.

6.

حَدَّثَنَا عُمَرُ بْنُ حَفْصِ بْنُ غِيَاثٍ: حَدَّثَنَا أَبِى: حَدَّثَنَا الأَعْمَشُ: حَدَّثَنَا خَيْثَمَةُ: حَدَّثَنَا سُوَيْدُ بْنُ غَفَلَةَ: قَالَ عَلِيٌّ ﷺ: إِذَا حَدَّثْتُكُمْ عَنْ رَسُولِ اللَّهِ ﷺ حديثًا، فَوَاَللَّهِ لأَنْ أَخِرَّ مِنَ السَّمَاءِ، أَحَبُّ إِلَيَّ مِنْ أَنْ أَكْذِبَ عَلَيْهِ، وَإِذَا حَدَّثْتُكُمْ فِيمَا بَيْنِى وَبَيْنَكُمْ، فَإِنَّ الْحَرْبَ خُدْعَةٌ، وَإِنِّى سَمِعْتُ رَسُولَ اللَّهِ ﷺ يَقُولُ: «سيخرج قَوْمٌ فِى آخِرِ الزَّمَانِ، أَحْدَاثُ الأَسْنَانِ، سُفَهَاءُ الأَحْلَامِ، يَقُولُونَ مِنْ خَيْرِ قَوْلِ الْبَرِيَّةِ، لَا يُجَاوِزُ إِيمَانُهُمْ حَنَاجِرَهُمْ، يَمْرُقُونَ مِنَ الدِّينِ كَمَا يَمْرُقُ السَّهْمُ مِنَ الرَّمِيَّةِ، فَأَيْنَمَا لَقِيتُمُوهُمْ فَاقْتُلُوهُمْ، فَإِنَّ فِى قَتْلِهِمْ أَجْرًا لِمَنْ قَتَلَهُمْ يَوْمَ الْقِيَامَةِ»

Sayyidina 'Alī ؓ said, "A people will come out at the end of times, immature (lit: with new teeth), foolish (lit. with foolish dreams). They will hold the discourse of the best of creation and recite Qur'an, but it will not go past their throats. They will passes through religion the way an arrow passes through its quarry. If you find them, kill them, for verily whoever kills them will have his reward from Allah on the Day of Judgment."[12]

7.

حَدَّثَنَا مُحَمَّدُ بْنُ جَعْفَرٍ، حَدَّثَنَا شُعْبَةُ، عَنْ حُمَيْدِ بْنِ هِلَالٍ، عَنْ عَبْدِ اللَّهِ بْنِ الصَّامِتِ، عَنْ أَبِى ذَرٍّ، عَنِ النَّبِيِّ ﷺ قَالَ: «إِنَّ أُنَاسًا مِنْ أُمَّتِى سِيمَاهُمُ التَّحْلِيقُ، يَقْرَءُونَ الْقُرْآنَ لَا يُجَاوِزُ حُلُوقَهُمْ، يَمْرُقُونَ مِنَ الدِّينِ كَمَا يَمْرُقُ السَّهْمُ مِنَ الرَّمِيَّةِ، هُمْ شَرُّ الْخَلْقِ وَالْخَلِيقَةِ.»

---

[12] Bukhārī, Muslim, al-Nasā'ī, Abū Dāwūd and Aḥmad.

The Prophet ﷺ said, “After me there will be people in my Community who recite the Qur'an. It will not go past their throats. They will pass through religion the way an arrow passes through its target. Then it does not return to it. They are the worst of human beings and the worst of all creation.”[13]

8.

عَنْ أَبِى هُرَيْرَةَ، أَنَّ رَسُولَ اللهِ ﷺ قَالَ: «رَأْسُ الْكُفْرِ نَحْوَ الْمَشْرِقِ، وَالْفَخْرُ وَالْخُيَلاَءُ فِى أَهْلِ الْخَيْلِ وَالإِبِلِ، الْفَدَّادِينَ أَهْلِ الْوَبَرِ، وَالسَّكِينَةُ فِى أَهْلِ الْغَنَمِ.»

The Prophet ﷺ said, “The head (or summit) of disbelief lies towards the east and the pride and arrogance lie in people who possess horses and camels who are also coarse - the boisterous (or noisy) people of the desert dwellers. Tranquility lies in people who possess sheep.”[14]

9.

عَنْ جَابِرِ بْنِ عَبْدِ اللَّهِ يَقُولُ: قَالَ رَسُولُ اللَّهِ ﷺ: «غَلَظَ الْقُلُوبِ، وَالجَفَاءُ فِى المَشْرِقِ، وَالإِيمَانُ فِى أَهْلِ الحِجَازِ»

The Prophet ﷺ said, “Harshness and dryness of heart are in the East [Najd], and true belief is amongst the people of Hijaz.”[15]

10.

عَنْ ابْنِ عُمَرَ قَالَ: ذَكَرَ النَّبِىُّ ﷺ فَقَالَ: «اللَّهُمَّ بَارِكْ لَنَا فِى شَامِنَا، اللَّهُمَّ بَارِكْ لَنَا فِى يَمَنِنَا». قَالُوا: وَفِى نَجْدِنَا؟ قَالَ: «اللَّهُمَّ بَارِكْ لَنَا فِى شَامِنَا، اللَّهُمَّ بَارِكْ

[13] Bukhārī, Abū Dāwūd, Ibn Mājah and Aḥmad.
[14] *Ṣaḥīḥ Bukhārī.*
[15] *Ṣaḥīḥ Muslim, Musnad Aḥmad, Ṣaḥīḥ Ibn Ḥibbān, al-Mu'jam al-Awsaṭ* of al-Ṭabarānī.

لَنَا فِي يَمَنِنَا». قَالُوا: يَا رَسُولَ اللّٰهِ، وَفِي نَجْدِنَا؟ قَالَ: «هُنَاكَ الزَّلَازِلُ وَالْفِتَنُ، وَبِهَا يَطْلُعُ قَرْنُ الشَّيْطَانِ »

Ibn ʿUmar ﷺ related that the Prophet ﷺ said, "O Allāh! Bless us in our Shām and our Yemen!" They said, "O Prophet of Allāh! And our Najd!" He did not reply, but again said, "O Allāh! Bless us in our Shām and our Yemen!" They said, "O Prophet of Allāh! And our Najd!" He did not reply, but again said, "O Allāh! Bless us in our Shām and our Yemen!" They said, "O Prophet of Allāh! And our Najd!" He said, "Thence shall come great upheavals and dissensions, and from it shall issue the horn of Shaytān." One narration has the addition, "And in it [Najd] are nine tenths of all evil."[16]

11. A version has, "The two epochs [or horns] of shaytan." Some scholars have said that the dual referred to Musaylima the Arch-liar and to Muḥammad ibn ʿAbd al-Wahhāb.

12. Some versions continue with the words: "And in it [Najd] is the consuming disease," i.e. death.

13. Some books of history mention the following version in the chapters devoted to the battles against the Banū Ḥanīfah:

يَخْرُجُ فِي آخِرِ الزَّمَانِ فِي بَلَدِ مُسَيْلِمَة رَجُلٌ يُغَيِّر دِينُ الإِسْلَام .

"At the end of times a man will come out of Musaylima's country and he will change the religion of Islam."

**Note:** Most of the Khawārij were from the Najd area, from the tribes of Banū Ḥanīfah, Banū Tamīm, and Wāʾil. Musaylimah al-Kadhdhāb [false prophet] was from the Banū Ḥanīfah, and Ibn ʿAbd al-Wahhāb is from Tamīm.

---

[16]Narrated from Ibn ʿUmar in *Ṣaḥīḥ Bukhārī* (4:390), *Ṣaḥīḥ Ibn Ḥibbān* (16:290), *Ṣaḥīḥ Muslim*, Tirmidhī, and Aḥmad with three chains, one of which with the addition: "And in it [Najd] are nine tenths of all evil."

13a.

أَنَّ وَادِيَهُم (وَادِى حَنِيفَه) لَا يَزَالُ وَادِى فُتِنٍ إِلَى آخِرِ الدَّهْرِ، وَلَا يَزَالُ فِى فِتْنَةٍ مِنْ كذابِهم إِلَى يَوْمِ الْقِيَامَةِ وَفِى رِوَايَةٍ «وَيْلٌ لليمامة وَيْلٌ لَا فِرَاقَ لَه».

Abū Bakr ؓ said concerning the Banū Ḥanīfah (the tribe of Musaylima the Liar): "Their valley [Najd] will not cease to be a valley of dissensions until the end of time, and the religion will never recover from their liars until Judgment Day," and in another version: "Woe to al-Yamāmah without end."[17]

13b.

حَدَّثَنَا مُحَمَّدُ بْنُ إِسْمَاعِيلَ الْخَلَّالِ، حَدَّثَنَا الْحَسَنُ بْنُ الْمُثَنَّى، أَخْبَرَنَا وَكِيعٌ، عَنْ عَاصِمِ بْنِ أَبِى النُّجُودِ، عَنْ أَبِى هُرَيْرَةَ ؓ، قَالَ رَسُولُ اللَّهِ ﷺ: «كَلَّا وَالَّذِى نَفْسِى بِيَدِهِ، إِنَّ مِنْهُمْ لِمَنْ هُوَ فِى أَصْلَابِ الرِّجَالِ لَمْ تَحْمِلْهُ النِّسَاءُ، وَلَيَكُنَّ آخِرُهُمْ مَعَ الْمَسِيحِ الدَّجَّالِ»

The Prophet ﷺ said, [and this is also narrated as when 'Alī ؓ killed the Khawārij, someone said: "Praise be to Allah Who has brought them down and relieved us from them." 'Alī ؓ replied: ] "Verily, by the One in Whose hand is my soul, some of them are still in the loins of men and they have not been born yet, and the last of them will fight on the side of the Antichrist."[18]

---

[17] Appears in Aḥmad Zaynī Daḥlān's *Ad-Durar al-Saniyyah fī Radd 'alā al-Wahhābiyyah*, without *isnad*, but supported by aḥādīth from Ibn Mas'ūd while the portion "Woe to al-Yamāmah without end" is part of a poem by Ziyād ibn Labīd reported by Ibn Mas'ūd regarding Musaylima and those directly affected by his falsehood, as related in *Al-Inshirāḥ fī Sīrat Abī Bakr* by al-Ṣallābī.

[18] *Musnad Aḥmad ibn Ḥanbal*, *Al-Muṣannaf* of Ibn Abī Shayba, and *Musnad Abū Ya'lā*.

14.

قَالَ عَبْدُ اللَّهِ بْنِ عمرو: سَمِعْتُ رَسُولَ اللَّهِ ﷺ يقول: «سيخرج نَاسٌ مِنْ أُمَّتِى مَنْ قِبَلِ الْمَشْرِقِ يَقْرَؤُون الْقُرْآنِ لَا يُجَاوِزُ تَرَاقِيَهُمْ كُلَّمَا خَرَجَ مِنْهُمْ قَرَن قطع كُلَّمَا خَرَجَ مِنْهُمْ قَرَن قطع» حَتَّى عَدَّهَا زِيَادَةً عَلَى عَشْرِ مَرَّاتٍ «كلما خَرَجَ قَرْن مِنْهُم قَطَع حَتَّى يَخْرُجَ الدَّجَّالُ فِى بقيتهم»

The Prophet ﷺ said, "A people that recite the Qur'an will come out of the East, but it will not go past their throats. Every time a generation of them is cut down another one will come until the last one finds itself on the side of the Antichrist."[19]

15.

عَنْ عَبْداللَّه بْنِ عُمَرَ قَالَ: قَالَ رَسُولُ اللَّهِ « ﷺإنها سَتَكُونُ فِتْنَةٌ تستنظف الْعَرَب ، قَتْلَاهَا فِى النَّارِ، اللِّسَان فِيهَا أَشَدُّ مِنْ وُقُوعِ السيف »

The Prophet ﷺ said, "There will be a huge confusion within my Community. There will not remain one house of the Arabs except that confusion will enter it. Those who die because of it are in the fire. The harm of the tongue in it will be greater than that of the sword."[20]

16.

وعن أبى هُرَيْرَةَ: أَنَّ رَسُولَ اللهِ ﷺ قَالَ: «سَتَكُونُ فِتْنَةٌ صَمَّاءُ، بَكْمَاءُ، عَمْيَاءُ، مَنْ أَشْرَفَ لَهَا اسْتَشْرَفَتْ لَهُ، وَإِشْرَافُ اللِّسَانِ فِيهَا كَوُقُوعِ السَّيْفِ»

[19] Bukhārī, *Musnad Aḥmad.*
[20] Tirmidhī and ibn Mājah.

The Prophet ﷺ said, "There will be a dissension (in which people will be) deaf, dumb and blind[21]: whoever tries to control it, the dissension will control him. And speaking out in it is like the striking of a sword."[22]

17.

سَيَظْهَر مِنْ نَجْدٍ شَيْطَانٌ تتزلزل جَزِيرَةِ الْعَرَبِ مِنْ فِتْنَتِهِ.

"A shaytan will appear in Najd by whose dissension the Arabian island will quake."[23]

18.

عَنْ أَبِى سَعِيدٍ الْخُدْرِيِّ رَضِىَ اللهُ عَنْهُ قَالَ : بَعَثَ عَلِيٌّ رَضِىَ اللهُ عَنْهُ وَهُوَ بِالْيَمَنِ بذهبة فِى تُرْبَتُهَا إِلَى رَسُولِ اللَّهِ ﷺ فَقَسَّمَهَا رَسُولُ اللَّهِ ﷺ بَيْنَ أَرْبَعَةَ نَفَرٍ «وفِيه» فَجَاءَ رَجُلٌ كَثَّ اللِّحْيَةِ مُشْرِف الْوَجْنَتَيْنِ غَائِرُ الْعَيْنَيْنِ نَاتِى الْجَبِين مَحْلُوق الرَّأْس فَقَال: « اتَّقِ اللَّهَ يَا مُحَمَّدُ فَقَالَ رَسُولُ اللَّهِ ﷺ : « فَمَن يُطِعْ اللَّهَ أَنْ عَصَيْتُه ؟ أيأمنُنى اللَّهُ عَلَى أَهْلِ الْأَرْضِ وَ لَا تأمنونى؟ » قَالَ ثُمَّ أَدْبَرَ الرَّجُلُ فستأذن رَجُلٌ مِنَ الْقَوْمِ فِى قتله (يَرَوْنَ أَنَّهُ خَالِدُ بْنُ الوليد) فَقَالَ رَسُولُ اللَّهِ ﷺ «أَنْ مَنْ ضِئْضِئِ هَذَا قَوْمٌ يَقْرَءُونَ الْقُرْآنَ لَا يُجَاوِزُ حَنَاجِرَهُمْ ، يَقْتُلُونَ أَهْلَ الْإِسْلَامِ وَيَدَعُونَ أَهْلَ الْأَوْثَانِ. يَمْرُقُونَ مِنْ الْإِسْلَامِ كَمَا يَمْرُقُ السَّهْمُ مِنْ الرَّمِيَّةِ، لَئِنْ أَنَا أَدْرَكْتُهُم لأقتلنهم قَتْلَ عَادٍ».

On the authority of Abū Saʿid al-Khudri ؓ that Sayyidina ʿAlī ؓ when he was in Yemen, sent gold in its dust to the Prophet ﷺ and

---

[21] Meaning people will be blind and unable to see the true issue nor listen to the voice of truth.

[22] Abū Dawūd.

[23] Aḥmad Zaynī ad-Dahlān in *Khulāṣat al-Kalām*.

the Prophet ﷺ divided it amongst four men. Then a man came who had a sunken eyes, bulging forehead, thick beard, fat raised cheeks, and clean-shaven head, and said, "O Muḥammad! Be afraid of Allah!" The Prophet ﷺ said, "Who would obey Allah if I disobeyed Him? (Allah). He trusts me over the people of the earth, but you do not trust me?" A man from the people (present then), who, I think, was Khālid ibn al-Walīd ؓ, asked for permission to kill him, but the Prophet ﷺ prevented him. When the man went away, the Prophet ﷺ said, "Verily in the wake of this time of mine comes a people who will recite Qur'an but it will not go past their throats. They will pass through religion the way an arrow passes through its quarry. They will kill the Muslims and leave the idolaters alone. If I saw them, verily I would kill them the way the tribe of ʻAd was killed [i.e. all of them]."[24]

19.

حَدَّثَنَا أَبُو بَكْرِ بْنُ أَبِى شَيْبَةَ، قَالَ: حَدَّثَنَا زَيْدُ بْنُ حُبَابٍ، عَنْ إِبْرَاهِيمَ بْنِ نَفِيرٍ، عَنْ أَبِيهِ، عَنْ أَبِى هُرَيْرَةَ، عَنْ رَسُولِ اللهِ ﷺ أَنَّهُ قَالَ : «سَيَكُونُ فِى آخِرِ الزَّمَانِ قَوْمٌ يُحَدِّثُونَكُم بِمَا لَمْ تَسْمَعُوا أَنْتُمْ وَلاَ آبَاؤُكُم فَإِيَّاكُمْ وَإِيَّاهُمْ، لاَ يُضِلُّونَكُمْ وَلاَ يَفْتِنُونَكُمْ»

The Prophet ﷺ said, "There will be towards the end of time a people who will say to you what neither you nor your forebears ever heard before. Beware of them lest they misguide you and bring you confusion."[25]

---

[24] *Ṣaḥīḥ Bukharī* and *Ṣaḥīḥ Muslim.*

[25] *Ṣaḥīḥ Muslim.*

20.

عَنْ عَلِيٍّ رَضِيَ اللهُ عَنْهُ قَالَ: سَمِعْتُ رَسُولَ اللهِ ﷺ يَقُولُ: «يَخْرُجُ قَوْمٌ مِنْ أُمَّتِي، يَقْرَءُونَ الْقُرْآنَ، لَا يُجَاوِزُ تَرَاقِيَهُمْ، يَمْرُقُونَ مِنَ الْإِسْلَامِ كَمَا يَمْرُقُ السَّهْمُ مِنَ الرَّمِيَّةِ، فَأَيْنَمَا لَقِيتُمُوهُمْ فَاقْتُلُوهُمْ، فَإِنَّ فِي قَتْلِهِمْ أَجْرًا لِمَنْ قَتَلَهُمْ يَوْمَ الْقِيَامَةِ»

The Prophet ﷺ said, "A group will emerge from my Ummah. They will recite the Qur'an, but it will not go beyond their throats. They will pass out of Islam just as an arrow passes through the prey. Wherever you encounter them, kill them, for in their killing there is a reward for the one who kills them on the Day of Judgment."[26]

21.

حَدَّثَنَا أَبُو بَكْرِ بْنُ أَبِي شَيْبَةَ، حَدَّثَنَا إِسْحَاقُ الأَزْرَقُ، عَنِ الأَعْمَشِ، عَنِ ابْنِ أَبِي أَوْفَى، قَالَ: قَالَ رَسُولُ اللَّهِ ﷺ: «نَّهُمْ كِلَابُ النَّارِ» قَالَ: قُلْتُ: «الأَزَارِقَةُ وَحْدَهُمْ أَمِ الْخَوَارِجُ كُلُّهَا؟» قَالَ: «بَلِ الْخَوَارِجُ كُلُّهَا»

'Abd Allāh ibn Abī Awfā ؓ said, "The Prophet of Allah ﷺ said: 'They are the dogs of the Fire.' I (the narrator) asked: "Is this limited to the Azāriqah[27] alone, or does it include all of the Khawārij?" He replied: "Rather, all of the Khawārij."[28]

---

[26] *Ṣaḥīḥ al-Bukhārī* and *Ṣaḥīḥ Muslim*.
[27] One of the most radical subsects of the Khawārij.
[28] *Musnad Aḥmad, Sunan Ibn Mājah, Kitāb al-Sunnah* of Ibn Abī 'Āṣim, and *Majma' al-Zawā'id*.

22.

عَنْ عَلِيٍّ ﵁ قَالَ: سَمِعْتُ رَسُولَ اللهِ ﷺ يَقُولُ: « يَخْرُجُ قَوْمٌ مِنْ أُمَّتِى، يَقْرَءُونَ
الْقُرْآنَ، لَيْسَتْ قِرَاءَتُكُمْ إِلَى قِرَاءَتِهِمْ بِشَيْءٍ، وَلَا صَلَاتُكُمْ إِلَى صَلَاتِهِمْ بِشَيْءٍ،
وَلَا صِيَامُكُمْ إِلَى صِيَامِهِمْ بِشَيْءٍ، يَقْرَءُونَ الْقُرْآنَ، يَحْسَبُونَ أَنَّهُ لَهُمْ وَهُوَ عَلَيْهِمْ،
لَا تُجَاوِزُ صَلَاتُهُمْ تَرَاقِيَهُمْ، يَمْرُقُونَ مِنَ الْإِسْلَامِ كَمَا يَمْرُقُ السَّهْمُ مِنَ الرَّمِيَّةِ، لَوْ
يَعْلَمُ الْجَيْشُ الَّذِينَ يُصِيبُونَهُمْ مَا قُضِيَ لَهُمْ عَلَى لِسَانِ نَبِيِّهِمْ ﷺ لَاتَّكَلُوا عَنِ
الْعَمَلِ، وَآيَةُ ذَلِكَ أَنَّ فِيهِمْ رَجُلًا لَهُ عَضُدٌ وَلَيْسَ لَهُ ذِرَاعٌ، عَلَى رَأْسِ عَضُدِهِ مِثْلُ
حَلَمَةِ الثَّدْيِ، عَلَيْهَا شَعَرَاتٌ بِيضٌ»

'Alī ibn Abī Ṭālib ﵁ related that the Prophet ﷺ said, "A group will emerge from my Ummah. They will recite the Qur'an, yet your recitation is nothing compared to theirs, nor your prayer to their prayer, nor your fasting to their fasting. They will recite the Qur'an thinking it is in their favor, but it is actually against them. Their prayer will not go beyond their collarbones. They will pass out of Islam as swiftly as an arrow passes through its target. If the army that confronts them knew what reward was decreed for them by the tongue of their Prophet ﷺ, they would rely upon that and abandon further deeds. And among them is a man with a malformed arm—no forearm—on the stump of which is a nipple-like growth, around which are white hairs."[29]

[29] *Ṣaḥīḥ Muslim* and *Sunan Abī Dāwūd*.

23.

حَدَّثَنَا مَحْمُودُ بْنُ غَيْلَانَ، حَدَّثَنَا عَبْدُ الرَّزَّاقِ، أَخْبَرَنَا مَعْمَرٌ، عَنْ هَمَّامِ بْنِ مُنَبِّهٍ، عَنْ أَبِى هُرَيْرَةَ، قَالَ: قَالَ رَسُولُ اللَّهِ ﷺ: «لَا تَقُومُ السَّاعَةُ حَتَّى يُنْبَعَثَ دَجَّالُونَ كَذَّابُونَ، قَرِيبٌ مِنْ ثَلَاثِينَ، كُلُّهُمْ يَزْعُمُ أَنَّهُ رَسُولُ اللَّهِ»

The Prophet ﷺ said, "The Hour will not be established until there arise thirty imposters (*dajjālūn*), each of whom will claim he is the prophet of Allah."[30]

24.

عَنْ أَبِى إِدْرِيسَ الْخَوْلَانِيِّ، أَنَّهُ سَمِعَ حُذَيْفَةَ بْنَ الْيَمَانِ ﷺ يَقُولُ: كَانَ النَّاسُ يَسْأَلُونَ رَسُولَ اللَّهِ ﷺ عَنِ الْخَيْرِ، وَكُنْتُ أَسْأَلُهُ عَنِ الشَّرِّ مَخَافَةَ أَنْ يُدْرِكَنِى، فَقُلْتُ: «يَا رَسُولَ اللَّهِ، إِنَّا كُنَّا فِى الْجَاهِلِيَّةِ وَشَرٍّ، فَجَاءَنَا اللَّهُ بِهَذَا الْخَيْرِ، فَهَلْ بَعْدَ هَذَا الْخَيْرِ مِنْ شَرٍّ؟» قَالَ: «نَعَمْ»

قُلْتُ: «وَهَلْ بَعْدَ ذَلِكَ الشَّرِّ مِنْ خَيْرٍ؟» قَالَ: «نَعَمْ، وَفِيهِ دَخَنٌ » قُلْتُ: «وَمَا دَخَنُهُ؟ » قَالَ: « قَوْمٌ يَهْدُونَ بِغَيْرِ هَدْيِى، تُعْرَفُ مِنْهُمْ وَتُنْكَرُ » قُلْتُ: « فَهَلْ بَعْدَ ذَلِكَ الْخَيْرِ مِنْ شَرٍّ؟ » قَالَ: «نَعَمْ، دُعَاةٌ عَلَى أَبْوَابِ جَهَنَّمَ، مَنْ أَجَابَهُمْ إِلَيْهَا قَذَفُوهُ فِيهَا» قُلْتُ: « يَا رَسُولَ اللَّهِ، صِفْهُمْ لَنَا » قَالَ: « هُمْ مِنْ جِلْدَتِنَا، وَيَتَكَلَّمُونَ بِأَلْسِنَتِنَا »

قُلْتُ: « فَمَا تَأْمُرُنِى إِنْ أَدْرَكَنِى ذَلِكَ »

---

[30] *Ṣaḥīḥ Bukhārī*, *Ṣaḥīḥ Muslim* and *Sunan al-Tirmidhī*.

قَالَ: « تَلْزَمُ جَمَاعَةَ الْمُسْلِمِينَ وَإِمَامَهُمْ » قُلْتُ: « فَإِنْ لَمْ يَكُنْ لَهُمْ جَمَاعَةٌ وَلَا إِمَامٌ؟» قَالَ: « فَاعْتَزِلْ تِلْكَ الْفِرَقَ كُلَّهَا، وَلَوْ أَنْ تَعَضَّ بِأَصْلِ شَجَرَةٍ، حَتَّى يُدْرِكَكَ الْمَوْتُ وَأَنْتَ عَلَى ذَلِكَ »

The Prophet ﷺ said, "Some people will be standing and calling at the gates of hell; whoever responds to their call, their will throw him into the Fire. They will be from our own people [i.e. Arabs] and will speak our language [Arabic]. Should you live to see them, stick to the main body (*jamaʿa*) of the Muslims and their leader. (If there is no main body and no leader,) isolate yourself from all these sects, even if you have to eat from the roots of trees until death overcomes you while you are in that state."[31]

25.

عَنْ جَابِرِ بْنِ سَمُرَةَ قَالَ: سَمِعْتُ رَسُولَ اللَّهِ ﷺ يَقُولُ: «أَنَّ بَيْنَ يَدَيْ السَّاعَةِ كَذَّابِيْنِ». قَالَ جَابِرٌ: «فَاحْذَرُوهُم»

The Prophet ﷺ said, "Just before the Hour there will be many liars." Jābir ibn Samurah said: "Be on your guard against them."[32]

26.

وَقَالَ أَحْمَدُ : عَنْ أَبِي عُثْمَانَ الْأَصْبَحِيّ ، سَمِعْتُ أَبَا هُرَيْرَةَ يَقُولُ : أَنَّ رَسُولَ اللَّهِ ﷺ قَالَ: « سَيَكُونُ فِي أُمَّتِي دَجَّالُونَ كَذَّابُونَ ، يَأْتُونَكُمْ بِبِدْعٍ مِنَ الْحَدِيثِ بِمَا لَمْ تَسْمَعُوا أَنْتُمْ وَلاَ آبَاؤُكُمْ ، فَإِيَّاكُمْ وَإِيَّاهُمْ ، لَا يفتنوكم »

The Prophet ﷺ said, "There will be Dajjals and liars among my Community. They will tell you something new, which neither

[31] *Ṣaḥīḥ Muslim.*

[32] *Ṣaḥīḥ Bukhārī* and *Ṣaḥīḥ Muslim.*

you nor your forefathers have heard. Be on your guard against them and do not let them lead you astray."[33]

27.

عَنْ أَبِى هُرَيْرَةَ قَالَ رَسُولُ اللَّهِ ﷺ : « قَبْلَ السَّاعَةِ سُنُون خِدَاعُه يَكْذِب فِيهَا الصَّادِقُ وَيُصَدَّقُ فِيهَا الْكَاذِبُ وَيُخَوَّنُ فِيهَا الأَمِينُ وَيُؤْتَمَنُ فِيهَا الْخَائِنُ وَيَنْطِقُ فِيهَا الرُّوَيْبِضَةُ» قَالَ « سُرَيْجٌ وَيَنْطِقُ فِيهَا الرُّوَيْبِضَةُ»

The Prophet ﷺ said, "The time of the Dajjal will be years of confusion. People will believe a liar, and disbelieve one who tells the truth. People will distrust one who is trustworthy, and trust one who is treacherous; and the *ruwaybiḍa* will have a say."[34] Someone asked: "Who are they?" He said: "Those who rebel against Allah and will have a say in general affairs."[35]

28.

أَن رجلاً سَأَلَ رَسُولَ اللَّهِ ﷺ عَنْ مَوْعِدِ قِيَامِ السَّاعَةِ فَقَالَ لَهُ رَسُولُ اللَّهِ ﷺ : «إِذَا ضُيِّعَتْ الأَمَانَةُ فَانْتَظِرِ السَّاعَةُ » قَالَ «كَيْفَ إِضَاعَتُهَا يَا رَسُولَ اللَّهِ » قَالَ إِذَا أُسْنِدَ الأَمْرُ إِلَى غَيْرِ أَهْلِهِ فَانْتَظِرِ السَّاعَةَ »

A man asked the Prophet of Allah ﷺ about the time of the coming of the Hour. The Prophet of Allah ﷺ replied: "When trust (*amānah*) is neglected, then await the Hour." The man asked: "How will it be neglected, O Messenger of Allah?" He answered: "When authority is entrusted to those who are unqualified, then await the Hour."[36]

---

[33] *Ṣaḥīḥ Bukhārī* and *Ṣaḥīḥ Muslim.*
[34] *Musnad Aḥmad* and Ibn Mājah.
[35] *Musnad Aḥmad* and Ibn Mājah.
[36] *Ṣaḥīḥ Bukhārī.*

29.

«...وأن تَرى الحُفاةَ العُراةَ العالةَ رِعاءَ الشَّاءِ يَتَطاوَلونَ فى البُنيانِ... »

[In a long hadith] the Prophet ﷺ said, "You will see the barefoot ones, the naked, the destitute, the shepherds and camelherds take pride in building tall structures in abundance."[37]

30.

عَنْ عَلِيِّ بْنِ أَبِى طَالِبٍ رَضِىَ اللهُ عَنْهُ قَالَ : « إِذَا رَأَيْتُمُ الرَّايَاتِ السُّودَ فَالْزَمُوا الْأَرْضَ فَلَا تُحَرِّكُوا أَيْدِيَكُمْ ، وَلَا أَرْجُلَكُمْ ، ثُمَّ يَظْهَرُ قَوْمٌ ضُعَفَاءُ لَا يُؤْبَهُ لَهُمْ ، قُلُوبُهُمْ كَزُبَرِ الْحَدِيدِ ، هُمْ أَصْحَابُ الدَّوْلَةِ ، لَا يَفُونَ بِعَهْدٍ وَلَا مِيثَاقٍ ، يَدْعُونَ إِلَى الْحَقِّ وَلَيْسُوا مِنْ أَهْلِهِ ، أَسْمَاؤُهُمُ الْكُنَى ، وَنِسْبَتُهُمُ الْقُرَى ، وَشُعُورُهُمْ مُرْخَاةٌ كَشُعُورِ النِّسَاءِ ، حَتَّى يَخْتَلِفُوا فِيمَا بَيْنَهُمْ ، ثُمَّ يُؤْتِى اللَّهُ الْحَقَّ مَنْ يَشَاءُ »

On the authority of ʻAlī ibn Abī Ṭālib ؓ: "When you see the black flags, then remain on the ground, and do not move your hands or your feet. Thereafter there shall emerge a weak folk to whom no concern is given. Their hearts will be like shards of iron. They shall be the people of the State (*Aṣ-ḥāb al-Dawla*). They will fulfil neither covenant nor agreement. They will invite to the Truth, though they are not from its people. Their names will be with '*kunā*'[38]and their ascriptions will be to villages (or places) [i.e., al-Misrī, al-Harranī, al-Baghdādī, etc.]. Their hair will be long like that of women. [They shall remain so] till they

[37] *Ṣaḥīḥ Bukhārī* and *Ṣaḥīḥ Muslim*.

[38] Plural form of *kunyā*; a teknonym in Arabic names. A *kunyā* is expressed by the use of 'Abū' that means 'father'.

differ among themselves, and then Allah will bring the truth to whomever He wills."[39]

31.

حَدَّثَنَا أَبُو كَامِلٍ، حَدَّثَنَا عَبْدُ الْوَاحِدِ، حَدَّثَنَا سُلَيْمَانُ الشَّيْبَانِيُّ، عَنْ يُسَيْرِ بْنِ عَمْرٍو، قَالَ: سَأَلْتُ سَهْلَ بْنَ حُنَيْفٍ، « هَلْ سَمِعْتَ النَّبِيَّ ﷺ يَذْكُرُ الْخَوَارِجَ؟ » فَقَالَ: سَمِعْتُهُ وَأَشَارَ بِيَدِهِ نَحْوَ الْمَشْرِقِ، «قَوْمٌ يَقْرَءُونَ الْقُرْآنَ بِأَلْسِنَتِهِمْ، لَا يَعْدُو تَرَاقِيَهُمْ، يَمْرُقُونَ مِنَ الدِّينِ كَمَا يَمْرُقُ السَّهْمُ مِنَ الرَّمِيَّةِ.»

From Yusayr ibn ʿAmr, who said: I asked Sahl ibn Ḥunayf: "Did you hear the Prophet ﷺ mention the Khawārij?" He replied: "I heard him, and he pointed with his hand toward the east, saying: 'A people who recite the Qurʾān with their tongues, but it does not go beyond their collarbones. They will exit the religion just as the arrow passes cleanly through the prey.'"[40]

32.

عَنْ أَبِي هُرَيْرَةَ، عَنِ النَّبِيِّ ﷺ أَنَّهُ قَالَ : «مَنْ خَرَجَ مِنَ الطَّاعَةِ ، وَفَارَقَ الْجَمَاعَةَ فَمَاتَ ، مَاتَ مِيتَةً جَاهِلِيَّةً ، وَمَنْ قَاتَلَ تَحْتَ رَايَةٍ عِمِّيَّةٍ يَغْضَبُ لِعَصَبَةٍ ، أَوْ يَدْعُو إِلَى عَصَبَةٍ ، أَوْ يَنْصُرُ عَصَبَةً ، فَقُتِلَ ، فَقِتْلَةٌ جَاهِلِيَّةٌ ، وَمَنْ خَرَجَ عَلَى أُمَّتِي ، يَضْرِبُ بَرَّهَا وَفَاجِرَهَا ، وَلَا يَتَحَاشَى مِنْ مُؤْمِنِهَا ، وَلَا يَفِي لِذِي عَهْدٍ عَهْدَهُ ، فَلَيْسَ مِنِّي وَلَسْتُ مِنْهُ »

The Prophet ﷺ said: "Whoever left off obedience and split the community and died, died the death of Ignorance. And whoever fought under the flag of the blind, becoming angry for partisanship and party spirit, or calling to partisanship, or

[39] Nuʿaym ibn Ḥammād, "Kitāb al-Fitan (Book of Tribulations)."
[40] *Ṣaḥīḥ Muslim.*

assisting partisanship, then is killed, he dies a death of Ignorance. And whoever comes against my Nation striking its good and its sinner with his sword and who does not seek out who its believers are and who does not fulfill his oath he is not from me and I am not from him."[41]

33.

عَنْ أَبِي بَكْرَةَ أَنَّ نَبِيَّ اللَّهِ ﷺ مَرَّ بِرَجُلٍ سَاجِدٍ وَهُوَ يَنْطَلِقُ إِلَى الصَّلَاةِ فَقَضَى الصَّلَاةَ وَرَجَعَ عَلَيْهِ وَهُوَ سَاجِدٌ فَقَالَ النَّبِيُّ ﷺ فَقَالَ: «مَنْ يَقْتُلْ هَذَا؟» فَقَامَ رَجُلٌ فَحَسِرَ عَنْ يَدَيْهِ فَاخْتَرَطَ سَيْفَهُ وَهَزَّهُ وَقَال : « يَا نَبِيَّ اللَّهِ بِأَبِي أَنْتَ وَأُمِّي كَيْفَ أَقْتُلُ رَجُلاً سَاجِدًا يَشْهَدُ أَنْ لَا إِلَهَ إِلَّا اللَّهُ وَأَنَّ مُحَمَّدًا عَبْدُهُ وَرَسُولُه ؟!» ثُمَّ قَال : « مَنْ يَقْتُلُ هَذَا؟» . فَقَامَ رَجُلٌ فَقَال : « أَنَا.» فَحَسِرَ عَنْ ذِرَاعَيْهِ وَاخْتَرَطَ سَيْفَهُ فَهَزَّهُ حَتَّى أَرْعَدَتْ يَدُهُ فَقَال:« يَا نَبِيَّ اللَّهِ كَيْفَ أَقْتُلُ رَجُلاً سَاجِدًا يَشْهَدُ أَنْ لَا إِلَهَ إِلَّا اللَّهُ وَأَنَّ مُحَمَّدًا عَبْدُهُ وَرَسُولُه ؟!» فَقَالَ النَّبِيُّ ﷺ : « وَالَّذِي نَفْسُ مُحَمَّدٍ بِيَدِهِ لَوْ قَتَلْتُمُوهُ لَكَانَ أَوَّلَ فِتْنَةٍ وَآخِرَه»

From Abī Bakra ﷺ that the Prophet ﷺ passed by a man prostrating and he was lengthening his prayers. He finished his [own] prayers and returned to him and he was still in prostration [*sajda*]. The Prophet ﷺ said, "Who will kill this man?" A man stood up, uncovered his arms, unsheathed his sword and shook it and said, "O Prophet of Allah, by the soul of my father and my mother, how can I kill a man in prostration who testifies that there is no God but Allah and Muḥammad is His servant and Messenger?"

The Prophet ﷺ repeated: "Who will kill this man?" Another man stood and said: "I will." He uncovered his forearms, unsheathed

[41] *Ṣaḥīḥ Muslim.*

his sword, and shook it until his hand trembled, then said: “O Prophet of Allah—how can I kill a man who is in prostration, bearing witness that there is no god but Allah and that Muḥammad is His servant and Messenger?”

The Prophet ﷺ said: “By the One in Whose Hand is the soul of Muḥammad if you had killed him it would have been the first *fitna* (tribulation) and its last.”[42]

34.

وَعَنْ أَبِى سَعِيدٍ الخُدْرِيِّ أَنَّ أَبَا بَكْرٍ الصِّدِّيقَ جَاءَ إِلَى النَّبِيِّ ﷺ فَقَالَ: يَا رَسُولَ اللَّهِ إِنِّى بِوَادٍ كَذَا وَكَذَا فَإِذَا رَجُلٌ مُتَخَشِّعٌ حَسَنُ الهَيْئَةِ يُصَلِّى. فَقَالَ لَهُ النَّبِيُّ ﷺ: « اذْهَبْ فَاقْتُلْه» قَالَ: فَذَهَبَ إِلَيْهِ أَبُو بَكْرٍ فَلَمَّا رَآهُ عَلَى تِلْكَ الحَالِ كَرِهَ أَنْ يَقْتُلَهُ فَرَجَعَ إِلَى رَسُولِ اللَّهِ ﷺ فَقَالَ النَّبِيُّ ﷺ لِعُمَرَ: « اذْهَبْ فَاقْتُلْه». فَذَهَبَ عُمَرُ فَرَآهُ عَلَى الحَالِ الَّذِى رَآهُ أَبُو بَكْرٍ فَرَجَعَ فَقَالَ: « يَا رَسُولَ اللَّهِ إِنِّى رَأَيْتُهُ يُصَلِّى مُتَخَشِّعًا فَكَرِهْتُ أَنْ أَقْتُلَهُ». قَالَ: « يَا عَلِيُّ اذْهَبْ فَاقْتُلْه». فَذَهَبَ عَلِيٌّ فَلَمْ يَرَهُ فَرَجَعَ عَلِيٌّ فَقَالَ: « يَا رَسُولَ اللَّهِ إِنِّى لَمْ أَرَه». قَالَ: فَقَالَ النَّبِيُّ ﷺ: « إِنَّ هَذَا وَأَصْحَابَهُ يَقْرَؤُونَ القُرْآنَ لَا يُجَاوِزُ تَرَاقِيَهُمْ يَمْرُقُونَ مِنَ الدِّيْنِ كَمَا يَمْرُقُ السَّهْمُ مِنَ الرَّمِيَةِ ثُمَّ لَا يَعُودُونَ فِيهِ حَتَّى يَعُودَ السَّهْمُ فِى فَوْقِهِ فَاقْتُلُوهُمْ هُمْ شَرُّ البَرِيَّةِ».

Abū Saʿīd al-Khuḍrī ؓ reported:

Abū Bakr al-Ṣiddīq ؓ came to the Prophet ﷺ and said, “O Messenger of Allah, I was in such-and-such a valley, and I saw a

[42] Sunan Abū Dāwūd, Aḥmad and al-Ṭabarānī.

man who appeared humble, well-groomed, and engaged in prayer." The Prophet ﷺ said, "Go and kill him."

Abū Bakr went, but when he saw the man in that condition, he disliked the idea of killing him and returned to the Prophet of Allah ﷺ. So the Prophet ﷺ said to ʿUmar ؓ: "Go and kill him."

ʿUmar went, saw the man as Abū Bakr had described him, and also returned, saying, "O Prophet of Allah, I saw him praying humbly, and I disliked killing him."

Then the Prophet ﷺ said to ʿAlī ؓ: "Go and kill him."

ʿAlī went but did not find him, and returned saying, "O Prophet of Allah, I did not see him."

The Prophet ﷺ then said: "Indeed, this man and his companions recite the Qurʾān, but it does not go beyond their collarbones. They exit the religion like an arrow passes through its target and never returns to it, unless the arrow returns to its bowstring. So kill them—they are the worst of creation."[43]

35.

وَعَنْ أَنَسِ بْنِ مَالِكٍ قَالَ: كَانَ رَجُلٌ عَلَى عَهْدِ رَسُولِ اللَّهِ ﷺ يَغْزُو مَعَ رَسُولِ اللَّهِ ﷺ، فَإِذَا رَجَعَ وَحَطَّ عَنْ رَاحِلَتِهِ عَمَدَ إِلَى مَسْجِدِ النَّبِيِّ، فَجَعَلَ يُصَلِّي فِيهِ فَيُطِيلُ الصَّلَاةَ، حَتَّى جَعَلَ أَصْحَابُ النَّبِيِّ ﷺ يَرَوْنَ أَنَّ لَهُ فَضْلًا عَلَيْهِمْ. فَمَرَّ يَوْمًا وَرَسُولُ اللَّهِ ﷺ قَاعِدٌ فِي أَصْحَابِهِ، فَقَالَ لَهُ بَعْضُ أَصْحَابِهِ: «يَا رَسُولَ اللَّهِ هُوَ ذَاكَ الرَّجُلُ». فَإِمَّا أَرْسَلَ إِلَيْهِ النَّبِيُّ ﷺ، وَإِمَّا جَاءَ مِنْ قِبَلِ نَفْسِهِ، فَلَمَّا رَآهُ رَسُولُ اللَّهِ ﷺ مُقْبِلًا،

[43] al-Ṭabarānī in *al-Muʿjam al-Kabīr* and Imām Aḥmad's *Musnad*; its narrators are trustworthy, *Musnad Abī Yaʿlā*,

قَالَ: «وَالَّذِي نَفْسِي بِيَدِهِ إِنَّ بَيْنَ عَيْنَيْهِ سُفْعَةً مِنَ الشَّيْطَانِ» . فَلَمَّا وَقَفَ عَلَى الْمَجْلِسِ، قَالَ لَهُ رَسُولُ اللَّهِ ﷺ: «أَقُلْتَ فِي نَفْسِكَ حِينَ وَقَفْتَ عَلَى الْمَجْلِسِ: لَيْسَ فِي الْقَوْمِ خَيْرٌ مِنِّي؟». قَالَ: «نَعَمْ »، ثُمَّ انْصَرَفَ فَأَتَى نَاحِيَةً مِنَ الْمَسْجِدِ فَخَطَّ خَطًّا بِرِجْلِهِ، ثُمَّ صَفَّ كَعْبَيْهِ، فَقَامَ يُصَلِّي. فَقَالَ رَسُولُ اللَّهِ ﷺ: «أَيُّكُمْ يَقُومُ إِلَى هَذَا فَيَقْتُلَهُ؟». فَقَامَ أَبُو بَكْرٍ، فَقَالَ رَسُولُ اللَّهِ ﷺ: «أَقَتَلْتَ الرَّجُلَ؟». فَقَالَ: «وَجَدْتُهُ يُصَلِّي فَهِبْتُهُ». فَقَالَ رَسُولُ اللَّهِ ﷺ: «أَيُّكُمْ يَقُومُ إِلَى هَذَا فَيَقْتُلَهُ؟». فَقَالَ عُمَرُ: «أَنَا». وَأَخَذَ السَّيْفَ، فَوَجَدَهُ يُصَلِّي فَرَجَعَ. فَقَالَ رَسُولُ اللَّهِ ﷺ لِعُمَرَ: «أَقَتَلْتَ الرَّجُلَ؟». فَقَالَ: «يَا رَسُولَ اللَّهِ وَجَدْتُهُ يُصَلِّي فَهِبْتُهُ» . فَقَالَ رَسُولُ اللَّهِ ﷺ: « أَيُّكُمْ يَقُومُ إِلَى هَذَا فَيَقْتُلَهُ؟». قَالَ عَلِيٌّ: «أَنَا» . فَقَالَ رَسُولُ اللَّهِ ﷺ: «أَنْتَ لَهُ إِنْ أَدْرَكْتَهُ» . فَذَهَبَ عَلِيٌّ فَلَمْ يَجِدْهُ. فَقَالَ رَسُولُ اللَّهِ ﷺ: « أَقَتَلْتَ الرَّجُلَ؟» . قَالَ: «لَمْ أَدْرِ أَيْنَ سَلَكَ مِنَ الأَرْضِ» . فَقَالَ رَسُولُ اللَّهِ ﷺ: «إِنَّ هَذَا أَوَّلُ قَرْنٍ خَرَجَ فِي أُمَّتِي». وَقَالَ رَسُولُ اللَّهِ ﷺ: «لَوْ قَتَلْتُهُ - أَوْ قَتَلَهُ - مَا اخْتَلَفَ فِي أُمَّتِي اثْنَانِ. إِنَّ بَنِي إِسْرَائِيلَ تَفَرَّقُوا عَلَى إِحْدَى وَسَبْعِينَ فِرْقَةً، وَإِنَّ هَذِهِ الأُمَّةَ - يَعْنِي أُمَّتَهُ - سَتَفْتَرِقُ عَلَى ثِنْتَيْنِ وَسَبْعِينَ فِرْقَةً، كُلُّهَا فِي النَّارِ إِلَّا فِرْقَةً وَاحِدَةً ». قُلْنَا: « يَا نَبِيَّ اللَّهِ مَنْ تِلْكَ الْفِرْقَةُ؟ » قَالَ: « الْجَمَاعَةُ ». قَالَ يَزِيدُ الرَّقَاشِيُّ: فَقُلْتُ لِأَنَسٍ: « يَا أَبَا حَمْزَةَ فَأَيْنَ الْجَمَاعَةُ؟ » قَالَ: « مَعَ أُمَرَائِكُمْ مَعَ

أُمَرَائِكُمْ ».

From Anas ibn Malik ﷺ who said:

There was a man in the time of the Prophet of Allah ﷺ who used to go to battle along with the Prophet of Allah ﷺ, so when he came back and alighted from his camel, he went to the mosque of the Prophet and began to pray and extended his prayers until the Companions of the Prophet of Allah ﷺ saw that he had a great virtue over them.

One day he passeed by the Prophet ﷺ who was sitting with his Companions, and some of his Companions said to him: "O the Prophet of Allah ﷺ! He is that man." so the Prophet ﷺ either sent for him or he came [to the Prophet ﷺ] from his own volition. When the Prophet ﷺ saw him before him he said, "by the One in Whose Hand is my soul, there is between his eyes the scorch mark of Satan."

So when he came to the gathering of the Prophet ﷺ the Prophet ﷺ said to him, "did you say to yourself, when you came before this gathering, there is no one among these people better than myself?"

He said, "Yes."

Then he left and he came to the end of the masjid where he made a line with his with his foot, then lined up his heels, so he stood praying, and the Prophet of Allah said: ﷺ said: "Which of you will stand up to this and kill him?" Abū Bakr as-Ṣiddīq: Prophet of Allah ﷺ said: "Did you kill the man?" He said: "I found him praying, so I let him get away." The Prophet of Allah ﷺ said: "Which of you will Who will kill him?" Umar said: "I will." And he took the sword and found him praying, so he returned. He said to Umar: "Did you kill the man?" He said, "O Prophet of Allah, I found him praying, so I left him be." The Prophet of Allah ﷺ said: said: "Which of you will stand up to this and kill him?"'Alī ﷺ said, "I will, O Prophet of Allah." The Prophet ﷺ said, "You are the one to do it, if you find him." So'Alī ﵁ went and did not find him. the Prophet ﷺ said, "did you kill the man?" He replied, 'I don't know where he went on this earth." The Prophet ﷺ said, "This is the first group [*qarn*] that has emerged in my Nation." Then the Prophet ﷺ said, "If you had killed him, there would never have been any differences among my Nation, for the Children of Israel split into seventy-one sects, and this nation, (meaning 'my Ummah'), shall split into seventy-two sects, all of them in Hell except one.'

We said, "O Prophet of Allah! Which group is that one?" He said, "The congregation (*al-jama'at*)." Yazīd al-Ruqāshī said, "I said to Anas [the narrator], 'O Aba Hamza! Where is the congregation?' He ﷺ said, 'With your leaders, with your leaders.'"[44]

36.

عَنْ أَبِى سَعِيدٍ الخُدْرِيّ رَضِىَ اللهُ عَنْهُ قَالَ: « بَيْنَا النَّبِىُّ ﷺ يَقْسِمُ ذَاتَ يَوْمٍ قَسْمًا، فَقَالَ ذُو الخُوَيْصِرَةِ رَجُلٌ مِنْ بَنِى تَمِيمٍ: « يَا رَسُولَ اللَّهِ، اَعْدِلْ. قَالَ: وَيَلْكِ، مَنْ يَعْدِلُ إِذَا لَمْ أُعْدَلْ؟ فَقَالَ عُمَرُ: ائْذَنْ لِى فَلَأَضْرِبَ عُنُقَهُ. قَالَ: لا، إِنَّ لَهُ أَصْحَابًا يَحْقِرُ أَحَدُكُمْ صَلاتَهُ مَعَ صَلاتِهِمْ، وَصِيَامَهُ مَعَ صِيَامِهِمْ. يَمْرُقُونَ مِنَ الدِّينِ كَمَرُوقِ السَّهْمِ مِنَ الرَّمِيَةِ. يَنْظُرُ إِلَى نَصْلِهِ فَلاَ يُوجَدُ فِيهِ شَىْءٌ، ثُمَّ يَنْظُرُ إِلَى رِصَافِهِ فَلاَ يُوجَدُ فِيهِ شَىْءٌ، ثُمَّ يَنْظُرُ إِلَى نَضِيِّهِ فَلاَ يُوجَدُ فِيهِ شَىْءٌ، ثُمَّ يَنْظُرُ إِلَى قُذَذِهِ فَلاَ يُوجَدُ فِيهِ شَىْءٌ، سَبْقُ الفَرْثِ وَالدَّمِ. يَخْرُجُونَ عَلَى حِينِ فِرْقَةٍ مِنَ النَّاسِ، آيَتُهُمْ رَجُلٌ إِحْدَى يَدَيْهِ مِثْلُ ثَدْىِ المَرْأَةِ، أَوْ مِثْلُ البَضْعَةِ

[44] *Musnad Abū Ya'ala*. Yazīd al-Ruqāshī was considered weak by most scholars.

تَدَرْدَرُ. قَالَ أَبُو سَعِيدٍ: أَشْهَدُ لَسَمِعْتُهُ مِنَ النَّبِيِّ ﷺ، وَأَشْهَدُ أَنِّي كُنْتُ مَعَ عَلِيٍّ حِينَ قَاتَلَهُمْ، فَالتُمِسَ فِى القَتْلَى فَأُتِيَ بِهِ عَلَى النَّعْتِ الَّذِى نَعَتَ النَّبِيُّ ﷺ.»

Abū Saʿīd narrated that while the Prophet ﷺ was distributing (something), ['Abdullah bin] Dhī al Khuwaysirah a man from Tamīm came and said, "Be just, O Allah's Apostle!" The Prophet ﷺ said, "Woe to you! Who would be just if I were not?" ʿUmar ibn al-Khaṭṭāb said, "Allow me to cut off his neck!" The Prophet ﷺ said, "Leave him, for he has companions, and if you compare your prayers with their prayers and your fasting with theirs, you will find your prayers and fasting insignificant in comparison to theirs. Yet they will pass out of the religion as an arrow darts through the prey in which case, if the shaft of the arrow is examined, nothing will be found on it, and when its blade is examined, nothing will be found on it; and then its rest is examined, nothing will be found on it. The arrow has been too fast to be smeared by dung and blood. The sign by which these people will be recognized will be a man whose one hand (or breast) will be like the breast of a woman (or like a moving piece of flesh). These people will appear when there will be differences among the people (Muslims)." Abū Saʿīd said: "I bear witness that I heard this hadith from the Prophet of Allah ﷺ, and I bear witness that ʿAlī ibn Abī Ṭālib fought them when I was with him. The man was sought and found and brought; he was just as the Prophet ﷺ had described him."[45]

37.

عَنْ مِقْسَمٍ مَوْلَى عَبْدِ اللَّهِ بْنِ الحَارِثِ بْنِ نَوْفَلٍ قَالَ: خَرَجْتُ أَنَا وَتَلِيدُ بْنُ كِلَابٍ اللَّيْثِيُّ حَتَّى أَتَيْنَا عَبْدَ اللَّهِ بْنَ عَمْرِو بْنِ العَاصِ وَهُوَ يَطُوفُ بِالبَيْتِ مُعَلِّقًا نَعْلَيْهِ بِيَدِهِ، فَقُلْنَا لَهُ: هَلْ حَضَرْتَ رَسُولَ اللَّهِ ﷺ حِينَ كَلَّمَهُ التَّمِيمِيُّ يَوْمَ

---

[45] Ṣaḥīḥ Bukhārī.

حُنَيْنٍ؟ قَالَ: نَعَمْ، أَقْبَلَ رَجُلٌ مِنْ بَنِى تَمِيمٍ يُقَالُ لَهُ: ذُو الخُوَيْصِرَةِ، فَوَقَفَ عَلَى رَسُولِ اللَّهِ ﷺ وَهُوَ يُعْطِى النَّاسَ، فَقَالَ: يَا مُحَمَّدُ قَدْ رَأَيْتُ مَا صَنَعْتَ مُنْذُ الْيَوْمِ فَقَالَ رَسُولُ اللَّهِ ﷺ: «أَجَلْ، فَكَيْفَ رَأَيْتَ؟» قَالَ: لَمْ أَرَكَ عَدَلْتَ. قَالَ: فَغَضِبَ رَسُولُ اللَّهِ ﷺ [ثُمَّ] قَالَ: «وَيْحَكَ، إِنْ لَمْ يَكُنِ الْعَدْلُ عِنْدِى فَعِنْدَ مَنْ يَكُونُ؟» فَقَالَ عُمَرُ بْنُ الخَطَّابِ رَحِمَهُ اللَّهُ: [يَا رَسُولَ اللَّهِ] أَلَا نَقْتُلُهُ؟ قَالَ: «لَا، دَعُوهُ فَإِنَّ لَهُ شِيعَةً يَتَعَمَّقُونَ فِى الدِّينِ حَتَّى يَخْرُجُوا مِنْهُ كَمَا يَخْرُجُ السَّهْمُ مِنَ الرَّمِيَّةِ، يُنْظَرُ فِى النَّصْلِ فَلَا يُوجَدُ شَىْءٌ، ثُمَّ فِى الْقَدَحِ فَلَا يُوجَدُ شَىْءٌ، ثُمَّ فِى الْفُوقِ فَلَا يُوجَدُ شَىْءٌ، سَبَقَ الْفَرْثَ وَالدَّمَ.»

Maqsim, the freed slave of 'Abdullāh ibn al-Ḥārith ibn Nūfal, reported: "I went out with Ṭālid ibn Kulāb al-Liṭī until we reached 'Abd Allāh ibn 'Amr ibn al-'Āṣ while he was circumambulating the Ka'bah, holding his sandals in his hand. We asked him, 'Were you present with the Prophet of Allah ﷺ, when the man from Banū Tamīm spoke to him on the day of Hunayn?' He said, 'Yes, a man from Banū Tamīm, called Dhī al Khuwaysirah, approached the Prophet of Allah ﷺ, while he was distributing (the spoils) to the people and said, "O Muḥammad, I have seen what you have done today." The Prophet of Allah ﷺ said, "Indeed, and how did you see it?" The man said, "I did not see you being just." The Prophet of Allah ﷺ, became angry and said, 'Woe to you! If justice is not with me, then with whom will it be?" 'Umar ibn al-Khaṭṭāb ؓ said, "O Prophet of Allah, shall we not kill him?" He said, "No, leave him, for he will have followers who will delve deeply into religion until they leave it, just as an arrow passes through its target. It is examined at the arrowhead and finds nothing, then at the shaft and finds nothing, then at the notch and finds nothing; it has outstripped the bowels and blood.'"" [46]

38.

وَعَنْ أَبِى سَعِيدٍ ؓ قَالَ: حَضَرْتُ رَسُولَ اللَّهِ ﷺ يَوْمَ حُنَيْنٍ وَهُوَ يُقَسِّمُ. قُلْتُ: فَذَكَرَ الْحَدِيثَ إِلَى أَنْ قَالَ: «عَلَامَتُهُمْ رَجُلٌ يَدُهُ كَثَدْيِ الْمَرْأَةِ كَالْبَضْعَةِ تَدَرْدَرُ فِيهَا شَعَرَاتٌ كَأَنَّهَا سُبْلَةُ سَبُعٍ».

قَالَ أَبُو سَعِيدٍ: فَحَضَرْتُ هَذَا مِنْ رَسُولِ اللَّهِ ﷺ يَوْمَ حُنَيْنٍ وَحَضَرْتُ مَعَ عَلِيٍّ حِينَ قَتَلَهُمْ بِنَهْرَوَانَ. قَالَ: «فَالْتَمَسَهُ عَلِيٌّ فَلَمْ يَجِدْهُ.»

قَالَ: «ثُمَّ وَجَدَهُ بَعْدَ ذَلِكَ تَحْتَ جِدَارٍ عَلَى هَذَا النَّعْتِ، فَقَالَ عَلِيٌّ: «أَيُّكُمْ يَعْرِفُ هَذَا؟» قَالَ رَجُلٌ مِنَ الْقَوْمِ: «نَحْنُ نَعْرِفُهُ، هَذَا حَرْقُوسٌ وَأُمُّهُ هُنَا».

قَالَ: «فَأَرْسَلَ عَلِيٌّ إِلَى أُمِّهِ» فَقَالَ: «مَنْ هَذَا» قَالَتْ: «مَا أَدْرِى يَا أَمِيرَ الْمُؤْمِنِينَ إِلَّا أَنِّى كُنْتُ أَرْعَى غَنَمًا لِى فِى الْجَاهِلِيَّةِ بِالرَّبَذَةِ فَغَشِيَنِى شَىْءٌ كَهَيْئَةِ الظُّلْمَةِ فَحَمَلْتُ مِنْهُ فَوَلَدْتُ هَذَا».

Abū Saʿīd ؓ said: "So I was present with the Prophet of Allah ﷺ on the day of Ḥunayn, and I was present with ʿAlī when he killed them in Nahrawān. He said: So ʿAlī searched for him and did not find him."

He said: "Then he found him after that under a wall with this description, so ʿAlī ؓ said: 'Which of you knows this one?' A man from the people said: 'We know him. This is Ḥarqūs and his mother is here.' He said: So ʿAlī ؓ sent for his mother and said: 'Who is this?' She said: 'I do not know, Commander of the

---

[46] Narrated by Aḥmad and al-Ṭabarānī in an abbreviated form, and the men in Aḥmad's chain are trustworthy.

Faithful, except that I was tending my sheep in the pre-Islamic era in Rabadha, and I was enveloped by something like darkness, so I conceived from it and gave birth to this [child].'"[47]

39.

عَن يَزِيدَ ابْنِ أَبِي صَالِحٍ أَنَّ أَبَا الوَضِيءِ عَبَّادًا حَدَّثَهُ قَالَ: كُنَّا فِي مَسِيرٍ عَامِدِينَ إِلَى الْكُوفَةِ مَعَ أَمِيرِ الْمُؤْمِنِينَ عَلِيِّ بْنِ أَبِي طَالِبٍ ﷺ، فَلَمَّا بَلَغْنَا مَسِيرَةَ لَيْلَتَيْنِ أَوْ ثَلَاثٍ مِنْ حَرُورَاءَ شَذَّ مِنَّا نَاسٌ، فَذَكَرْنَا ذَلِكَ لِعَلِيٍّ، فَقَالَ: « لَا يَهُولَنَّكُمْ أَمْرُهُمْ فَإِنَّهُمْ سَيَرْجِعُونَ »، فَنَزَلْنَا، فَلَمَّا كَانَ مِنَ الْغَدِ شَذَّ مَثْلَىٰ مَنْ شَذَّ، فَذَكَرْنَا ذَلِكَ لِعَلِيٍّ، فَقَالَ: « لَا يَهُولَنَّكُمْ أَمْرُهُمْ فَإِنَّ أَمْرَهُمْ يَسِيرٌ ». وَقَالَ عَلِيٌّ ﷺ: «لَا تَبْدَأُوهُمْ بِقِتَالٍ حَتَّى يَكُونُوا هُمُ الَّذِينَ يَبْدَأُونَكُمْ.» فَجَثَوْا عَلَى رُكَبِهِمْ وَاتَّقَيْنَا بِتُرُسِنَا، فَجَعَلُوا يُنَاوِلُونَا بِالنُّشَّابِ وَالسِّهَامِ، ثُمَّ إِنَّهُمْ دَنَوْا مِنَّا، فَأَسْنَدُوا لَنَا الرِّمَاحَ، ثُمَّ تَنَاوَلُونَا بِالسُّيُوفِ، حَتَّى هَمُّوا أَنْ يَضَعُوا السُّيُوفَ فِينَا. فَخَرَجَ إِلَيْهِمْ رَجُلٌ مِنْ عَبْدِ الْقَيْسِ يُقَالُ لَهُ: صَعْصَعَةُ بْنُ صُوحَانَ، فَنَادَى ثَلَاثًا فَقَالُوا: «مَا تَشَاءُ؟» فَقَالَ: « أُذَكِّرُكُمُ اللهَ أَنْ تَخْرُجُوا بِأَرْضٍ تَكُونُ مَسَبَّةً عَلَى أَهْلِ الْأَرْضِ، وَأُذَكِّرُكُمُ اللهَ أَنْ تَمْرُقُوا مِنَ الدِّينِ مُرُوقَ السَّهْمِ مِنَ الرَّمِيَّةِ.» فَلَمَّا رَأَيْنَاهُمْ قَدْ وَضَعُوا فِينَا السُّيُوفَ، قَالَ عَلِيٌّ ﷺ: «انْهَضُوا عَلَى بَرَكَةِ اللهِ تَعَالَى »، فَمَا كَانَ إِلَّا فَوَاقٌ مِنْ نَهَارٍ، حَتَّى ضَجَعْنَا مَنْ ضَجَعْنَا وَهَرَبَ مَنْ هَرَبَ.

---

[47] It was narrated in *Musnad Abī Ya'là* at length, and it includes Abū Ma'shar Nujayḥ, who is weak.

فَحَمِدَ اللّٰهَ عَلِيٌّ ﷺ، فَقَالَ: «إِنَّ خَلِيلِي ﷺ أَخْبَرَنِي: «أَنَّ قَائِدَ هَؤُلَاءِ رَجُلٌ مُخَدَّجُ الْيَدِ عَلَى حَلَمَةِ ثَدْيِهِ شُعَيْرَاتٌ كَأَنَّهُنَّ ذَنَبُ يَرْبُوعٍ فَالْتَمِسُوهُ »، فَالْتَمَسُوهُ فَلَمْ يَجِدُوهُ، فَأَتَيْنَاهُ، فَقُلْنَا: «إِنَّا لَمْ نَجِدْهُ »، فَقَالَ: «الْتَمِسُوهُ، فَوَاللّٰهِ مَا كَذَبْتُ وَلَا كُذِبْتُ ». فَمَا زِلْنَا نَلْتَمِسُهُ حَتَّى جَاءَ عَلِيٌّ بِنَفْسِهِ إِلَى آخِرِ الْمَعْرَكَةِ الَّتِي كَانَتْ لَهُمْ، فَمَا زَالَ يَقُولُ: «اقْلِبُوا ذَا، اقْلِبُوا ذَا »، حَتَّى جَاءَ رَجُلٌ مِنْ أَهْلِ الْكُوفَةِ، فَقَالَ: « هَا هُوَ ذَا».

فَقَالَ عَلِيٌّ: «اللّٰهُ أَكْبَرُ، وَاللّٰهِ لَا يَأْتِيكُمْ أَحَدٌ يُخْبِرُكُمْ مَنْ أَبُوهُ مَلَكٌ »، فَجَعَلَ النَّاسُ يَقُولُونَ: «هَذَا مَلَكٌ هَذَا مَلَكٌ »، يَقُولُ عَلِيٌّ: «ابْنُ مَنْ؟» يَقُولُونَ: «لَا نَدْرِي» فَجَاءَ رَجُلٌ مِنْ أَهْلِ الْكُوفَةِ، فَقَالَ: «أَنَا أَعْلَمُ النَّاسِ بِهَذَا»، كُنْتُ أَرُوضُ مُهْرَةً لِفُلَانِ بْنِ فُلَانٍ شَيْخٌ مِنْ بَنِي فُلَانٍ، وَأَضَعُ عَلَى ظَهْرِهَا جَوَالِقَ سَهْلَةً أُقْبِلُ بِهَا وَأُدْبِرُ إِذْ نَفَرَتِ الْمُهْرَةُ فَنَادَانِي»، فَقَالَ: «يَا غُلَامُ انْظُرْ، فَإِنَّ الْمُهْرَةَ قَدْ نَفَرَتْ»، فَقُلْتُ: «إِنِّي لَأَرَى خَيَالًا كَأَنَّهُ غَرْبٌ أَوْ شَاةٌ، إِذْ أَشْرَفَ هَذَا عَلَيْنَا»، فَقَالَ: «مَنِ الرَّجُلُ؟» فَقَالَ: «رَجُلٌ مِنْ أَهْلِ الْيَمَامَةِ»، قَالَ: «وَمَا جَاءَ بِكَ شَعِثًا شَاحِبًا؟» قَالَ: «جِئْتُ أَعْبُدُ اللّٰهَ فِي مُصَلَّى الْكُوفَةِ»، فَأَخَذَ بِيَدِهِ مَا لَنَا رَابِعٌ إِلَّا اللّٰهُ، حَتَّى انْطَلَقَ بِهِ إِلَى الْبَيْتِ، فَقَالَ لِامْرَأَتِهِ: « إِنَّ اللّٰهَ تَعَالَى قَدْ سَاقَ إِلَيْكِ خَيْرًا»، قَالَتْ: « وَاللّٰهِ إِنِّي إِلَيْهِ لَفَقِيرَةٌ، فَمَا ذَلِكَ؟» قَالَ:« هَذَا الرَّجُلُ شَعِثٌ شَاحِبٌ كَمَا تَرَيْنَ، جَاءَ مِنَ الْيَمَامَةِ لِيَعْبُدَ اللّٰهَ فِي مُصَلَّى الْكُوفَةِ»، فَكَانَ يَعْبُدُ اللّٰهَ فِيهِ وَيَدْعُو النَّاسَ حَتَّى اجْتَمَعَ النَّاسُ إِلَيْهِ.

فَقَالَ عَلِيٌّ: «أَمَا إِنَّ خَلِيلِي ﷺ أَخْبَرَنِي أَنَّهُمْ ثَلَاثَةُ إِخْوَةٍ مِنَ الْجِنِّ، هَذَا أَكْبَرُهُمْ، وَالثَّانِي لَهُ جَمْعٌ كَثِيرٌ، وَالثَّالِثُ فِيهِ ضَعْفٌ»

On the authority of Yazīd ibn Abī Ṣāliḥ that Abū al-Waḍī' 'Abbād narrated to him: "We were traveling toward Kūfa with the Commander of the Faithful, 'Alī ibn Abī Ṭālib ﷺ. When we reached a distance of two or three nights' journey from Ḥarūrā', some men broke away from us. We mentioned this to 'Alī, and he said: 'Let not their matter alarm you, for they will return.'

The next day, twice as many people broke away. We mentioned it again, and he said: 'Do not be disturbed by their situation, for their affair is of little consequence.'

'Alī then said: 'Do not initiate fighting against them until they begin aggression against you.'

They knelt on their knees, and we shielded ourselves with our shields. They began attacking us with arrows and spears, then advanced closer with lances, and finally struck at us with swords—until they nearly managed to pierce our ranks.

Then a man from 'Abd al-Qays, named Ṣa'ṣa'ah ibn Ṣūḥān, came forward and called out three times. They said: 'What do you want?' He replied: 'I remind you by Allah: do not depart upon a path that would bring disgrace upon the people of this land. And I remind you by Allah: do not depart from the religion as an arrow passes through its prey.'[48] When we saw they had indeed turned their swords upon us, 'Alī said: 'Advance, with the blessing of Allah Most High.'

And it was no more than a brief span of the day before we had felled those who were meant to die, and those who remained had fled. Then 'Alī praised Allah and said: 'Verily, my beloved ﷺ informed me: "The leader of these people is a man with a

---

[48] A reference to the hadiths 21, 33, 38 mentioned above.

maimed hand, upon his nipple there are small hairs like the tail of a jerboa—so seek him out.'"

We searched for him but did not find him. We went back to 'Alī and said: 'We did not find him.' He said: 'Search again, for by Allah, I neither lied nor was lied to.' We continued searching until 'Alī himself came to the final battlefield and kept saying: 'Turn this one over. Turn this one over.' Until a man from Kūfa called out: 'Here he is.'

Then 'Alī said: '*Allāhu akbar*! By Allah, no one shall inform you of this except one whose father was an angel.'

The people began to say: 'This is an angel! This is an angel!'

'Alī asked: 'Who is his father?' They said: 'We do not know.'

Then a man from Kūfa said: 'I am the most knowledgeable about him. I used to train a mare for a shaykh from such-and-such a tribe. I would ride it and dismount, when the mare spooked and he called to me, saying: "Young man! Look—the mare has bolted!"

I said: "I see a shadow—it looks like a raven or a sheep." Then that one approached us and asked: "Who is this man?" They said: "A man from al-Yamāmah." He said: "Why have you come, so disheveled and pale?" He replied: "I came to worship Allah in the masjid of Kūfa."

He took him by the hand—none was with them except Allah—and went with him to the house. He said to his wife: "Allah Most High has brought you great goodness." She replied: "By Allah, I am in need of it. What is it?" He said: "This man—disheveled and pale as you see—came from al-Yamāmah to worship Allah in the masjid of Kūfa. And he remained there, worshipping Allah and calling people, until the people gathered around him."'

ʿAlī then said: ʿIndeed, my beloved ﷺ informed me: they are three brothers from among the jinn—this is the eldest, the second commands many, and the third is weak.'"[49]

40.

أَخْبَرَنَا أَبُو النُّعْمَانِ حَدَّثَنَا حَمَّادُ بْنُ زَيْدٍ عَنْ يَزِيدَ بْنِ حَازِمٍ قَالَ حَدَّثَنِى عَمِّى جَرِيرُ بْنُ زَيْدٍ أَنَّهُ سَمِعَ تُبَيْعًا يُحَدِّثُ عَنْ كَعْبٍ قَالَ إِنِّى لأَجِدُ نَعْتَ قَوْمٍ يَتَعَلَّمُونَ لِغَيْرِ الْعَمَلِ وَيَتَفَقَّهُونَ لِغَيْرِ الْعِبَادَةِ وَيَطْلُبُونَ الدُّنْيَا بِعَمَلِ الآخِرَةِ وَيَلْبَسُونَ جُلُودَ الضَّأْنِ وَقُلُوبُهُمْ أَمَرُّ مِنَ الصَّبْرِ فَبِى يَغْتَرُّونَ أَوْ إِيَّاىَ يُخَادِعُونَ فَحَلَفْتُ بِى لأُتِيحَنَّ لَهُمْ فِتْنَةً تَتْرُكُ الْحَلِيمَ فِيهَا حَيْرَانَ .

Abū al-Nuʿmān told us: Ḥammād ibn Zayd narrated to us from Yazīd ibn Hāzim, who said: My uncle Jarīr ibn Zayd told me that he heard Tubayʿ, narrating from Kaʿb, who said: "I find the description of a people who learn without acting, who seek knowledge without worship, who seek worldly gains through the actions of the Hereafter, and who wear the skins of sheep, but their hearts are harsher than aloes. Do they deceive Me or attempt to deceive Me? I have sworn by Myself that I will send them a trial that will leave even the wise among them confused.'"[50]

---

[49] It was narrated in *Kitāb al-Sunnah* by ʿAbd Allāh ibn Aḥmad ibn Ḥanbal, and al-Hakim in *al-Mustadrak ʿala al-Ṣaḥīḥayn*, and its narrators are trustworthy. It was also narrated in *Muṣannaf Ibn Abī Shaybah*, Ṭabarī's *Tārīkh* and Ibn Saʿd's *Ṭabaqāt.*

[50] *Sunan al-Dārimī,* graded *ṣaḥīḥ*.

# Jamīl Effendī Al-Zahāwī's
# *al-Fajr al-ṣādiq fī al-radd ʿalā munkiri al-tawassul wa al-khawāriq*

## "The True Dawn: A Refutation of Those Who Deny the Validity of Using Means to Allah and the Miracles of Saints"

## 1: The Origin of the Wahhābi Sect

The Wahhābiyya is a sect whose origin can be traced back to Muḥammad Ibn ʿAbd al-Wahhāb. Although he first came on the scene in 1143 (1730 CE), the subversive current his false doctrine initiated took some fifty years to spread. It first showed up in Najd. This is the same district that produced the false prophet, Musaylima in the early days of Islam. Muḥammad Ibn Saʿūd, governor of this district, aided Ibn ʿAbd al-Wahhāb's effort, forcing people to follow him. One Arab tribe after another allowed itself to be deceived until sedition became commonplace in the region, his notoriety grew and his power soon passed beyond anyone's control. The nomadic Arabs of the surrounding desert feared him. He used to say to the people: "I call upon you but to confess *tawḥīd* (monotheism) and to avoid *shirk* (associating partners with Allah in worship)." The people of the countryside followed him and where he walked, they walked until his dominance increased.

Muḥammad Ibn ʿAbd al-Wahhāb was born in 1111 and died in 1207 (1699-1792 CE). At the outset of his career, he used to go back and forth to Mecca and Madina in quest of knowledge. In Madina, he studied with Shaykh Muḥammad Ibn Sulaimān al-Kurdī and Shaykh Muḥammad Ḥayāt al-Sindī (d. 1750). These two shaykhs as well as others with whom he studied early on detected the heresy of Ibn ʿAbd al-Wahhāb's creed. They used to say: "Allah will allow him be led astray; but even unhappier will be the lot of those misled by him." Circumstances had reached this state when his father ʿAbd al-Wahhāb, a pious scholars of the religion, detected heresy in his belief and began to warn others about his son. His own brother Sulayman soon followed suit, going so far as to write a book entitled *al-Sawāʿiq* (the thunderbolts)[51] to refute the innovative and subversive creed manufactured by Ibn ʿAbd al-Wahhāb.

Famous writers of the day made a point of noting the similarity between Ibn ʿAbd al-Wahhāb's beginnings and those of the false prophets prominent in Islam's initial epoch like Musaylima the Prevaricator, Sajāḥ al-Aswad al-ʿAnsīyy, Ṭulayḥah al-Asadīyy and others of their kind.[52] What was different in ʿAbd al-Wahhāb's case was his concealment in himself of any outright claim to prophecy. Undoubtedly, he was unable to gain support enough to openly proclaim it. Nevertheless, he would call those who came from abroad to join his movement *Muhājirūn* and those who came from his own region *Anṣār* in patent imitation of those who took flight from Mecca with the Prophet Muḥammad ﷺ in contrast to the inhabitants of Madina at the start of Islam. Ibn ʿAbd al-Wahhāb habitually ordered anyone who had already made the obligatory Pilgrimage (Hajj) to Mecca prior joining him to remake it since Allah had not accepted it the first time they performed because they had done so as unbelievers. He was also given to telling people wishing to enter his religion: "You must bear witness against yourself that you were a disbeliever and you must bear witness against your parents that they were disbelievers and died as such."

His practice was to declare a group of famous scholars of the past unbelievers. If a potential recruit to his movement agreed

---

[51]Sulaimān ibn ʿAbd al-Wahhāb al-Najdī, *al-Ṣawāʿiq al-Ilāhiyyah fī al-radd ʿalā al-Wahhābiyyah* ["Divine Lightnings in Refuting the Wahhabis"], ed. Ibrāhīm Muḥammad al-Baṭāwī (Cairo: Dār al-Insān, 1987). Offset reprint by Waqf Ikhlas, Istanbul: Hakikat Kitabevi, 1994.

[52]These were self-declared prophets in the time of the Prophet ﷺ and directly after.

and testified to the truth of that declaration, he was accepted; if not, an order was given and he was summarily put to death. Ibn ʿAbd al-Wahhāb made no secret of his view that the Muslim community had existed for the last six hundred years in a state of unbelief (*kufr*) and he said the same of whoever did not follow him. Even if a person was the most pious and Allah-fearing of Muslims, he would denounce them as idolaters (*mushrikun*), thus making the shedding of their blood and confiscation of their wealth licit (*ḥalāl*).

On the other hand, he affirmed the faith of anyone who followed him even though they be persons of most notoriously corrupt and profligate styles of life . He played always on a single theme: the dignity to which Allah had entitled him. This directly corresponded to the decreased reverence he claimed was due the Prophet whose status as Messenger he frequently depreciated using language fit to describe an errand boy rather than a divinely commissioned apostle of faith. He would say such things as "I looked up the account of Ḥudaybiyya and found it to contain this or that lie." He was in the habit of using contemptuous speech of this kind to the point that one follower felt free to say in his actual presence: "This stick in my hand is better than Muḥammad because it benefits me by enabling me to walk. But Muḥammad is dead and benefits me not at all". This, of course, expresses nothing less than disbelief and counts legally as such in the fours schools of Islamic law.[53]

Returning always to the same theme, Ibn ʿAbd al-Wahhāb used to say that prayer for the Prophet ﷺ was reprehensible and disliked (*makrūh*) in the Shariʿa. He would prohibit blessings on the Prophet ﷺ from being recited on the eve of Friday prayer and their public utterance from the minbar, and punish harshly

[53]It is an offense passible of death to disparage the Prophet ﷺ in all Four Schools according to the *ijma*ʿ. See the chapters on disparaging the Prophet ﷺ in Qāḍī ʿIyāḍ's *al-Ṣārim al-Maslūl ʿalā Shātim al-Rasūl,* Ibn Qunfudh's *al-Wasīlah ilā al-Islām bi-al-Nabiyy*, etc.

anyone who pronounced such blessings. He even went so far as to kill a blind *mu'adhdhin* (caller to prayer) who did not cease and desist when he commanded him to abandon praying for the Prophet ﷺ in the conclusion to his call to prayer. He deceived his followers by saying that all that was done to keep monotheism pure.

At the same time, he burned many books containing prayers for the Prophet ﷺ, among them *Dalā'il al-Khayrāt* and others, similar in content and theme. In this fashion, he destroyed countless books on Islamic law, commentary on the Qur'an, and the science of hadith whose common fault lay in their contradiction of his own vacuous creed. While doing this, however, he never ceased encouraging any follower to interpret Qur'an and hadith for himself and to execute this informed only by the light of his own understanding, darkened though it be through errant belief and heretical indoctrination.

Ibn 'Abd al-Wahhāb clung fiercely to denouncing people as unbelievers. To do this he used Qur'anic verses originally revealed about idolaters and extended their application to monotheists. It has been narrated by 'Abd Allāh Ibn 'Umar ؇ and recorded by Imam Bukhārī in his book of sound hadiths that the Khawārij transferred the Qur'anic verses meant to refer to unbelievers and made them refer to believers.[54] He also relates another narration transmitted on the authority of Ibn 'Umar whereby the Prophet ﷺ, on him be peace, said: "What I most fear in my community is a man who interprets verses of the Qur'an out of context." The latter hadith and the one preceding it apply to the case of Ibn 'Abd al-Wahhāb and his followers.

It is obvious the intention to found a new religion lay behind his statements and actions. In consequence, the only thing he accepted from the religion of our Prophet, on him be peace was the Qur'an. Yet even this was a matter of surface show. It

---

[54]Bukhārī, English ed. 9:50.

allowed people to be ignorant of what his aims really were. Indicating this is the way he and his followers used to interpret the Qur'an according to their own whim and ignore the commentary provided by the Prophet ﷺ, on him be peace, his Companions, the pious predecessors of our Faith (*al-salaf al-ṣāliḥūn*), and the Imams of Qur'anic commentary. He did not argue on the strength of the narrations of the Prophet ﷺ and sayings of the Companions, the Successors to the Companions and the Imams among those who derived rulings in the Shariʿa by means of *Ijtihād* nor did he adjudicate legal cases on the basis of the principle sources (*uṣūl*) of the Shariʿa; that is, he did not adhere to Consensus (*ijmāʿ*) nor to sound analogy (*qiyās*). Although he claimed to belong to the legal school (*madhhab*) of Imam Aḥmad Ibn Ḥanbal, this pretense was motivated by falsehood and dissimulation. The scholars and jurists of the Hanbali school rejected his multifarious errors. They wrote numerous articles refuting him including his brother whose book touching on Ibn ʿAbd al-Wahhāb's errors was mentioned earlier.

The learned al-Sayyid al-Ḥaddād al-ʿAlawī[55] said: "In our opinion, the one element in the statements and actions of Ibn ʿAbd al-Wahhāb that makes his departure from the foundations of Islam unquestionable is the fact that he, without support of any generally accepted interpretation of Qur'an or Sunna (*bi-lā taʾwīl*), takes matters in our religion necessarily well-known to be objects of prohibition (*ḥarām*) agreed upon by consensus (*ijmaʿ*) and makes them permissible (*ḥalāl*).[56] Furthermore, along with that he disparages the Prophets, the messengers, saints and the pious. Willful disparagement of anyone failing under these categories of person is unbelief (*kufr*) according to the consensus reached by the four Imams of the schools of Islamic law.

---

[55]This is the father of al-Ḥabīb Aḥmad Mashhur al-Ḥaddād who died in Mecca in 1995—may Allah have mercy on both of them.

[56]E.g. asking Muslims to repeat their *shahāda*, testification of faith, or killing them.

Then he wrote an essay called "The Clarification of Unclarity Concerning the Creator of Heaven and Earth" (*Kashf al-shubuhāt ʿan Khāliq al-arḍ wa-l-samāwāt*)[57] for Ibn Saʿūd. In this work he declared that all present-day Muslims are disbelievers and have been so for the last six hundred years. He applied the verses in the Qur'an, meant to refer to disbelievers among the tribe of the Quraysh to most Allah-fearing and pious individuals of the Muslim community. Ibn Saʿūd naturally took this work as a pretext and device for extending his political sovereignty by subjecting the Arabs to his dominance. Ibn ʿAbd al-Wahhāb began to call people to his religion and instilled in their hearts the idea that every one under the sun was an idolater. What's more, anyone who slew an idolater, when he died, would go immediately to paradise.

As a consequence, Ibn Saʿūd carried out whatever Ibn ʿAbd al-Wahhāb ordered. If he commanded him to kill someone and seize his property, he hastened to do just that. Indeed, Ibn ʿAbd al-Wahhāb sat among his folk like a prophet in the midst of his community. His people did not forsake one jot or little of what he told them to do and acted only as he commanded, magnifying him to the highest degree and honoring him in every conceivable way. The clans and tribes of the Arabs continued to magnify him in this manner until, by that means, the dominion of Ibn Saʿūd increased far and wide as well as that of his sons after him.

The Sharif of Mecca, Ghālib, waged war against Ibn Saʿūd for fifteen years until he grew too old and weak to fight. No one remained if his supporters except they joined the side of his foe. It was then that Ibn Saʿūd entered Mecca in a negotiated peace settlement in the year 1220 (1805 CE). There he abided for some seven years until the Sublime Porte[58] raised a military force

---

[57]Edited by ʿAbd Allāh ibn ʿAbd al-Raḥmān Al Bassām, 1st ed. (Cairo: Dār Iḥyāʾ al-Kutub al-ʿArabīyah, 1377 [1957 or 1958]).

[58] 'Sublime Porte' refers to the central government of the Ottoman Empire, especially its foreign affairs office and the imperial court in Istanbul.

addressing command to its minister, the honorable Muḥammad ʿAlī Pashā, ruler of Egypt. His intrepid army advanced against Ibn Saʿūd and cleared the land of him and his followers. Then, he summoned his son Ibrāhīm Pashā who arrived in the district in the year 1233 (1818 CE). He finished off what remained of them.

Among the hideous abominations of Ibn ʿAbd al-Wahhāb was his prohibiting people from visiting the tomb of the Prophet ﷺ. After his prohibition, a group went out from Ahsa to visit the Prophet ﷺ. When they returned, they passed by Ibn ʿAbd al-Wahhāb in the district and he commanded that their beards be shaved and they be saddled on their mounts backwards to return in this fashion to Ahsa. The Prophet ﷺ, related information about those Khawārij preserved in numerous hadiths. Indeed, these sayings constitute one of the signs of his prophethood; for they convey knowledge of the unseen. Among them are his statements in Bukhārī and Muslim: "Discord there; discord there!" pointing to the East; and "A people will come out of the East who will read Qur'an with it not getting past their throats. They will pass through the religion like an arrow when it passes clean through the flesh of its quarry and comes back pristine and prepared to be shot once again from the bow. They will bear a sign in the shaving of their heads." Another narration of the hadith adds: "They are calamity for the whole of Allah's creation; Blessed is he who kills them" or "Slay them! For though they appeal to Allah's Book, they have no share therein." He said: "O Allah! bless us in our Syria and bless us in our Yemen!" They said: "O Prophet of Allah! And in our Najd?" but he replied: "In Najd will occur earthquakes and discords; in it will dawn the epoch [or horn] of Shaytan." Again he said: "A people will come out of the East, reading the Qur'an and yet it will not get past their throats. Whenever one generation is cut off, another arises until the last dawns with the coming of Antichrist. They will bear a sign in the shaving of their heads."

Now the Prophet's ﷺ words explicitly specify in text his reference to those people coming out of the East, following Ibn ʿAbd al-Wahhāb in the innovations he made in Islam. For they were in the habit of ordering those who followed them to shave their heads and once they began to follow them, they did not abandon this practice. In none of the sects of the past prior to that of Ibn ʿAbd al-Wahhāb did the likes of this practice occur.[59] He even ordered the women who followed him to shave their heads. Once he ordered a woman who entered his new religion to shave her head. She replied: "If you ordered men to shave off their beards, then it would be permissible for you to order a woman to shave her head. But the hair on a woman's head has the same sacred status as a man's beard." Ibn ʿAbd al-Wahhāb was unable to answer her.

Found among the narrations transmitted from the Prophet ﷺ is his statement: "At the end of time, a man will rise up in the same region from which once rose Musaylima. He would change the religion of Islam." Another saying has it: "From Najd a Shaytan will appear on the scene causing the Arab peninsula to erupt in earthquake from discord and strife."

One of the abominations of Ibn ʿAbd al-Wahhāb was his burning of books containing works of Islamic science and his slaughter of the scholars of our faith and people both of the top classes and common people. He made the shedding of their blood and confiscation of their property and wealth licit well as digging up graves of *awlīyā* (saints). In al-Aḥsā, for example, he ordered

[59]The mufti of Zabīd (Yemen), al-Sayyid ʿAbd al-Raḥmān al-Ahdal, said: "It is enough testimony against Muḥammad ibn ʿAbd al-Wahhāb that the Prophet ﷺ said: *'Their mark is that they shave,'* for this was never done by any of the sects of innovators before him."
Related by al-Sayyid Aḥmad Dahlān in his book *Khulāṣat al-Kalām fī Bayān ʾUmarāʾ al-Balad al-Ḥarām*, p. 235.
When Ibn ʿAbd al-Wahhāb had a group of Muslims killed because they did not shave their heads as he required his followers to do, al-Munʿamī wrote a lampoon whose first verse is::

*Afī ḥalq al-raʾs bil-sakākīn wal-ḥaddī*
*ḥadīthun ṣaḥīḥun bil-ʾasānīd ʿan jaddī*

[Is there, concerning shaving the head at swordpoint,
an authentic hadith related from my ancestor the Prophet ﷺ?]

that some of the graves of *awlīyā* be used by people to relieve the wants of nature. He forbade people to read Imam Jazūlī's *Dalā'il al-Khayrāt*, to perform supererogatory acts of devotion, to utter the names of Allah in His remembrance, to read the mawlid celebrating the Prophet's birth, or to evoke blessings and prayers on the Prophet ﷺ from the minaret after the call to prayer. What's more, he killed whoever dared to do any of those things. He forbade any kind of act of worship after the canonical prayers. He would publicly declare a Muslim a disbeliever for requesting a prophet, angel or individual of saintly life to join his or her prayers to that person's own prayer expressing some intention whose fulfillment might be asked of Allah as, for example, when one supplicates the Creator for the sake of Muḥammad, on him be peace, to accomplish such-and-such a need. He also said anyone who addressed a person as lord or master (*sayyid*) was a disbeliever.

Undoubtedly, one of the worst abominations perpetrated by the Wahhābis under the leadership of Ibn ʿAbd al-Wahhāb was the massacre of the people of al-Ṭāʾif. upon entering that town. They killed everyone in sight, slaughtering both child and adult, the ruler and the ruled, the lowly and well-born. They began with a suckling child nursing at his mother's breast and moved on to a group studying Qur'an, slaying them, down to the last man. And when they wiped out the people they found in the houses, they went out into the streets, the shops and the mosques, killing whoever happened to be there. They killed even men bowed in prayer until they had annihilated every Muslim who dwelt in Ṭāʾif and only a remnant, some twenty or more, remained.

These were holed up in Beit al-Fitni with ammunition, inaccessible to their approach. There was another group at Beit al-Far to the number of two-hundred and seventy who fought them that day, then the second and third until the Wahhābis sent them a guarantee of clemency; only they tendered this proposal as a trick. For when they entered, they seized their weapons and slew them to a man. Others, they also brought out with a guarantee of clemency and a pact to the valley of Waj where they abandoned them in the cold and snow, barefoot, naked, exposed in shame with their women, accustomed to the privacy afforded them by common decency and religious morality. They, then, plundered their possessions: wealth of any kind, household furnishings and cash.

They cast books into the streets alleys and byways to be blown to and fro by the wind among which could be found copies of the Qur'an, volumes of Bukhārī, Muslim, other canonical collections of hadith and books of fiqh, all mounting to the thousands. These books remained there for several days, trampled upon by the Wahhābis. What's more, no one among them made the slightest attempt to remove even one page of Qur'an from under foot to preserve it from the ignominy of this display of disrespect. Then, they razed the houses and made what was once a town a barren waste land. That was in the year 1217 (1802 CE).

## 2: The Wahhābis and their Recent Rebellion (1905)

The leader of the Wahhābis at the time of the present account is ʿAbd al-Raḥmān Ibn Fayṣal, one of the sons of Muḥammad Ibn Saʿūd, the Rebel who turned his face in disobedience to the greater Islamic Caliphate in the year 1205 (1790 CE). The incidents he occasioned with the Sharif of Mecca, Ghālib continued up to 1220 (1805 CE). Then, when the Sharif's power to do battle with him waned, the Sublime Porte raised a military force against him, charging its minister the late Muḥammad ʿAlī Pāsha, ruler of Egypt, and his son, the late Ibrahim Pashā, with its command as we pointed out in the preceding chapter just as books of history have written it down.

Now this ʿAbd al-Raḥmān was for almost thirty years governor of Riyadh. Then, Muḥammad Ibn al-Rashid, took over Najd as its governor and Ibn Saʿūd fled to the remote areas by the sea coast. He ultimately ended up in Kuwait where he remained in humiliating poverty. Nor did anyone feel sorry for him until the Sublime Porte looked on him with favor and afforded him a remittance. Thereupon, he began to live a more comfortable life, though in a state of exile, due to the largesse of the Ottoman government.

When Muḥammad ibn al-Rashīd died—may Allah have mercy on his soul—his nephew came to power, ʻAbd al-ʻAzīz ibn Mutʻib ibn al-Rashīd, who is governor of Najd at the time of writing this.

It fell out that an incident took place between the aforementioned ʻAbd al-ʻAzīz and the Shaykh of Kuwait, Mubārak ibn Ṣabāḥ. Behind it was Mubārak ibn Ṣabāḥ's murder of his brother, Muḥammad ibn Ṣabāḥ, who was, at that time, *locum tenens* or temporary substitute of the Sublime Porte in Kuwait. The same individual also murdered his other brother and robbed his children of an immense inheritance. The latter heirs, thereupon, fled the fratricide's further pursuit. Faced with this state affairs, the uncle of the murdered children, Yusuf Ibn Ibrāhīm, took refuge with ʻAbd al-ʻAzīz Ibn al-Rashīd, the Governor of Najd, taking sides in his presence against his own brother Mubārak ibn Ṣabāḥ, the aforementioned fratricide, in an attempt get back the wealth the latter had robbed from his nephews.

Negotiations of reconciliation broke down to the point that each of the two parties in the dispute fitted out an army, one against the other. The two armies clashed at a place called Tarafiya. Mubārak ibn Ṣabāḥ suffered defeat and some four thousands fighters from his army were killed, although he escaped unharmed. He fled back to Kuwait vanquished and humiliated. However, no time elapsed before ibn Ṣabāḥ sought foreign protection and rebelled again. The foreigners supplied both money and arms. Then, the power of ʻAbd al-Raḥmān ibn Fayṣal ibn Saʻūd began to wax strong against the Governor of Najd, al-Rashid. It chanced that the latter was at that moment preoccupied by military expeditions in the remote districts of Riyadh.

Mubārak ibn Ṣabāḥ seized his opportunity. Helped by foreigners with money and weapons, he fitted out an army and placed it under the command of that ʻAbd al-Raḥmān mentioned earlier. Ibn Ṣabāḥ dispatched him to Riyadh to capture it, occupy it by force, fortify its barriers and entrench himself within. When the news of what had happened reached the governor, Ibn al-Rashīd, he returned and encircled it for a time with the intent of taking it back. His encampment around Riyadh lasted for a year. Then, something occurred in one of remote areas of the district that distracted him from the encirclement and he abandoned it. This afforded Ibn Saʻūd an opportunity as well, for he came out with his army outfitted with foreign aid and seized ʻUnayza, Burayda, and the remainder of the regions of Qusaym.

The Sublime Porte witnessed the hostile action of ʻAbd al-Raḥmān, his rebellion and insolence against its friend the faithful Governor of Najd, Ibn al-Rashīd, as well as his defection to the foreigner, it dispatched a squadron from its intrepid armies as a support for the Governor of Najd, Ibn al-Rashīd to cut off the rear end of those renegades and crush their hostile activities. Ibn al-Rashid snuffed out the sparks of sedition. The Ottoman forces clashed with the rebels, the party of Ibn Saʻūd near the town of Bahkrama in the region of Qusaym. A fierce battle between the two forces ensued, issuing finally in the defeat of the rebellious party, the forces of Ibn Saʻūd. The victorious army took possession of eleven standards of their defeated foe. Ibn al-Rashid and his soldiers were extolled for their role in crushing the enemy in this battle and their bravery; the memory of it will last forever. This praise has an undeniable base in fact, word and deed. [At the time of writing this,] the vanquished are presently enclosed and surrounded with the intrepid forces of Ibrāhīm Pashā looking on and encompassing them round about, praised for their exemplary manner of containing the enemy and curbing his defiance.

## 3: The Wahhābi Creed

When Ibn ʻAbd al-Wahhāb saw that the inhabitants of the rural regions of Najd were different from the urbane world of its cities, he would extol the simplicity and innocence of human beings as they are found in the primordial state of the Arabs. Ignorance, then, gained the upper hand among the city-dwellers so that sciences of an intellectual character lost status in their eyes. Besides, there was no longer an appetite in their hearts for things sound and wholesome, once he had sewn in their hearts the seeds of corruption and vice. For it was to vice and corruption that his own soul had become attuned since time immemorial nourished by his grab at political leadership masked under the name of religion. After all, he believed—May Allah revile him—that prophethood was only a matter of political leadership which the cleverest people attain when circumstances help them in the form of an ignorant and uninformed crowd.

Moreover, since Allah the Exalted had shut tight the door of prophecy after the Seal of the Prophets, our master Muḥammad ﷺ, on him be Allah's blessing and peace, there was no way to realize the goal of his desires except to claim that he was a renewer of the faith (*mujaddid*) and an independent thinker in the formulation of legal rulings (*Mujtahid*). Such an attitude—or rather the worst and most profound state of moral misguidance and religious disbelief --brought him to the point of declaring every group of Muslims disbelievers and idolaters. For he set out to apply the verses of Qur'an specifically revealed to single out the idolaters of the Arabs to generally include all Muslims who visit the grave of their Prophet, and seek his intercession with their Lord.

In doing this, he cast aside what ran counter to his own invalid claims and the vain desires commanding his ego to work mischief regarding the explicit statements of the Master of all messengers and Imams, the *Mujtahid*s of our religion (that is, who have the capacity to exercise independent reasoning in the process of legal discovery). Hence, when he saw a consensus of legal opinion in matters of faith which clashed with his own unwarranted innovations, he rejected it as a matter of principle, asserting: "I do not entertain any opinion of people coming after the Qur'an which contains all that pertains to Islam, the fresh and the dry (cf. 6:59)." Thus, he failed to heed what the Qur'an itself declared, when it says:

﴿ وَيَتَّبِعْ غَيْرَ سَبِيلِ ٱلْمُؤْمِنِينَ ﴾

*He who follows the path of those other than the Muslims'*[60]

inasmuch as he accepted from Qur'an only what it reveals concerning the idolaters of the Arabs. These verses he interpreted in his own obscure fashion, having the gall to stand before Allah and facilitate the accomplishment of his own personal political ambitions by means of an unwarranted and unjustified exegesis of His holy text. His method here mostly consisted in applying these verses concerning the idolaters to Muslims and on this basis declaring that they had been disbeliever for the last six hundred years, that one may shed their blood with impunity and confiscate their property and reduce their land, the Abode of Peace, (*Dār al-Islām*) to a field of war against disbelief (*Dār al-Ḥarb*).

Yet the Prophet ﷺ, on him be Allah's blessings and peace, from what we see in the two canonical collections of sound hadith, Bukhārī and Muslim, declared in the narration where the angel Jibril assumes human form to question him about the creed of Islam: "Islam is to testify that there is no god but Allah and Muḥammad is the Messenger of Allah." Again, in the narration of 'Umar he says: "Islam is built upon five articles of faith (the first being): "Testimony that there is no god but Allah, Muḥammad is His servant and Messenger." Then, there is his declaration to the delegation of 'Abd al-Qays also cited in Bukhārī and Muslim: "I am commanding you to believe in Allah alone. Do you know what belief in Allah alone is? It is to testify: 'There is no god but Allah and Muḥammad is the Messenger of Allah.'" Also cited is his exhortation: "I have been ordered to fight people until they say: 'There is no god but Allah

60 Sūratu 'n-Nisā [Women], 4:115.

and that Muḥammad is the Messenger of Allah.'" Finally, the Prophet ﷺ says: "It is sufficient that folk say: 'There is no god but Allah.'"

However, Ibn 'Abd al-Wahhāb and his followers go counter to all these statements of the Prophet ﷺ. They make a disbeliever the one who says: "There is no god but Allah and Muḥammad is the Messenger of Allah" because that person is not like them in respect to their claim that the one who testifies in the aforementioned fashion and yet asks Allah for something for the sake of a prophet or evokes the name of someone absent or dead or makes a vow to that person it is as if his belief diverges from his testimony. His only aim here is to market goods unsaleable where sound hadiths and correct exegeses of the Qur'an are exchanged. We will explain—Allah willing—the groundlessness of this claim and show its spuriousness to the reader.

It is amazing how Ibn 'Abd al-Wahhāb misrepresents use of the Prophet's ﷺ name in petitions to Allah or *tawassul* under the pretense of monotheism (*tawḥīd*) and divine transcendence (*tanzīh*) claiming that use of a prophet's name in this manner constitutes association of a partner with Allah; yet at the same time there is his outright assertion to the effect that Allah's mounting His throne is like sitting on it and his affirmation that Allah has a hand, face and possesses spatial dimension! He says it is possible to point to Him in the sky and claims that He literally descends to the lower heavens so that he gives a body to Allah who is too exalted in the height of His sublimity beyond what obscurantists proclaim. What happens to Divine transcendence after making Allah a body so that the lowliest of inanimate creatures share properties in common with their Creator? To what is He, the Exalted, transcendent when He is characterized in so deprecating a fashion and His divinity couched in terms so redolent of ridicule and contempt?

One of Ibn 'Abd al-Wahhāb's more enormous stupidities is this: When he sees reason going against his claims, he casts aside all modesty and suspends reason giving it no role in his judgment.

He endeavors thereby to make people like dumb beasts when it comes to matters of faith. He prohibits reason to enter into religious affairs despite the fact that there is no contradiction between reason and faith. On the contrary, whenever human minds reach their full measure of completeness and perfection, religion's merits and prerogatives with regard to reason become totally manifest. Is there in this age, an age of the mind's progress, anything more abominable than denying reason its proper scope, especially when the cardinal pivot of religion and the capacity to perform its duties is based on the ability to reason? For the obligation to carry out the duties of Islam falls away when mental capacity is absent. Allah has addressed his servants in many places in the Qur'an: يَٰٓأُوْلِي ٱلۡأَلۡبَٰبِ *"O you who possess understanding"* (cf. 65:10) alerting them to the fact that knowledge of the realities of religion is only a function of those possessed of minds.

Now the time has come for me to give a summation of the vain and empty prattle of the renegade Wahhābi sect which it aspires to issue as a doctrine. Next, I shall discuss it in terms of the research that has been brought in its rebuttal and refute its argument. Their invalid creed consists of a number of articles:

(1) Affirming the face, hand, and spatial direction of the Creator and making Him a body that descends and ascends;

(2) Making principles derived from narration (*naql*) prior to those derived from reason (*ʿaql*);

(3) Denial and rejection of consensus as a principle (*aṣl*) of Shariʿa legislation;

(4) Similar denial and rejection of analogy (*qiyās*);

(5) Not permitting copying and emulating the judgments of the Imams who have in Islam the status of those capable of exercising independent reasoning in matters of Shariʿa;

(6) Declaring Muslims who contradict them disbelievers;

(7) Prohibition of using the name of the Messenger in petitions to Allah or the name of someone else among the friends of Allah and the pious;

(8) Making the visiting of the tombs of prophets and of pious people illicit;

(9) Declaring a Muslim a disbeliever who makes a vow to someone other than Allah or sacrifices at the grave or final resting place of *awlīyā* or the pious.

## 4: Their Making Allah Into A Body (*Tajsīm*)

Although the Wahhābis declare any Muslim a disbeliever who visits the Prophet's grave and asks Allah for help by means of him, and they consider that associating with Him a partner in his Divinity, declaring that His Divinity is too transcendent for that, they at the same time annul this transcendence when they insist on making his "firm establishment on His throne" at once:

- a literal affirmation of the throne,
- a taking up a spatial position with respect to it, and
- being physically situated at a higher level above it.

They further corrupt divine transcendence by making Him a holder of the heavens in one finger, the earth in another, the trees in another, and the angels in yet another. Then, they affirm of Him spatial direction placing Him above the heavens fixed upon the throne so a person can to point to Him in a sensible fashion. Also, they say that he literally descends to the lower heavens and ascends from thence. Accordingly, one of them recites:

*"If affirming Allah's establishment on His throne*
*means He is body, then I make Him a body!*
*If affirming His attributes is making Him like something,*
*then I do not hesitate to make Him like something!*
*If denying establishment on His throne, or His attributes,*
*or His speech is to avoid anthropomorphism*
*Then I deny that our Lord avoids anthropomorphism!*
*He alone grants success,*
*and He knows best and is more sublime."*

Now I shall relate to you the way at least one of the Wahhābiyya expresses his doctrine in a book entitled *The Pure and Undefiled Religion.*[61] The author says that by body one means either what is made up of matter and form according to the philosophers; or what is composed of the atom according to the theologians. All this, he says, is categorically denied of Allah, the Exalted. But the correct view—he says—denies it of contingent[62] beings as well; for neither are the bodies of creatures composed of matter and form nor of atom. Note how far off the beaten track and eccentric his mode of expression is here. For, on the one hand, he claims that in its generally accepted meaning "body" is either a hylomorphic[63] or an atomic compound. On the other hand, he rejects the existence of "body" in this sense whether the body in question be necessary[64] or contingent. Evidently, the purpose of this denial is to arrive at a denial of corporeality. This follows from his own opinion concerning Allah: since he does not want it said that he likens the Creator to the creature, he denies corporeality to the creature but only in the sense of a hylomorphic or atomic compound, taking it for granted that the reader will be cognizant of the fact no body is made up purely of matter and form—as the philosophers have it.

But, then, he is left with it being composed of atoms. Yet his ignorance does not lie in the strange claim that "body" possesses no limit at which it ends.[65] It is no wonder that he arrives at this abominable confusion. I wish he had explained, after his denial of body's being a hylomorphic compound, what order of bodily composition he has in mind. I do not think even his muddle-headedness allows him to hold to the claim that bodies are made up of infinitely divisible parts. The *'Ulamā' of Kalām* or dialectical theologians reject this position without exception.

[61]Muḥammad Ṣiddīq Ḥasan, Nawāb of Bhopāl (1832–1890), author of *al-Dīn al-Khāliṣ* in 4 volumes (Cairo: Maktabat Dār al-'Urūbah, 1956–1960).
[62]I.e. created.
[63]I.e. composed of both corporeal and spiritual matter.
[64]I.e. non-created.
[65]I.e. it lies in graver conclusions yet.

Today's science denies it as well. Besides, any demonstrative proof one can produce will vouchsafe its invalidity. To delve into an explanation of why this is so would take us beyond our proper business.

So to return to the present discussion, we note that the Wahhābi author, casting his first definition aside, goes on to say that if one means by body what is characterized by attributes and means by this that bodies see by means of vision, talk, speak, hear, are pleased, are angry, then these are ideas affirmed of the Lord, the Exalted, as well insofar as one ascribes such attributes to Him. Hence, to characterize bodies as seeing, hearing, etc. cannot constitute denial of the same attributes to Him.

I reply: We know of no one who defines body as something which talks, speaks, hears, sees, which is pleased and is angry. These attributes exist only in a living being possessed of intelligence. To be sure, the body sees by means of vision just as he says. But his affirmation of body to Allah in this sense is to bring Him down to the level of His creatures because of what it simultaneously denies about His Divinity. When predicated of Allah, being a body in this sense is an imperfection and deficiency which is obligatorily rejected.

As from the standpoint of reason, according to the scientific explanation given in optics, sight is only brought about by the radiation of light on the surface of a visible object and the reflection of light-rays on the organ of vision. Given this, we must first suppose the existence of an object of vision which possesses, as we said, a surface on which light-rays fall. And that, in turn, requires an object made up of parts. But here we take a fall, if our purpose is to characterize Divinity. This is because the body in this sense is identical to the definition of "body" which the Wahhābi author of "The Pure and Undefiled Religion" denies is true of Allah at the outset. Indeed, he denies that body in this sense applies to any contingent (*mumkin*) being.

From the standpoint of transmitted proof-texts Allah says:

﴿ لَا تُدْرِكُهُ الأَبْصَارُ وَهُوَ يُدْرِكُ الأَبْصَارَ ﴾

*Sight does not perceive Him yet He perceives sight.*[66]

There is no conflict of this verse with the verse:

﴿ وُجُوهٌ يَوْمَئِذٍ نَّاضِرَةٌ ﴾

*Faces on that day will be bright looking at their Lord.*[67]

For the mode of this vision of Him on the day of resurrection is unknown just as true doctrine teaches and proclaims. It is possible that vision on that day consists of a kind of uncovering without a need of sight which is, strictly speaking, without parallel. Indeed, the text's use of "faces" signifies precisely that inasmuch as He did not say eyes. And its saying "bright" expresses clearly the occurrence of the perfected attitude experienced by the faces as a result of that unveiling.

Then he says "If you mean by body what can be pointed to in a sensible fashion then the most knowing of Allah among His creatures pointed to Him by his finger raising it up to the sky,"[68] etc. then I reply that common sense judges that what is pointed to in a sensible way must be in a direction and a place and must be an object of vision—and all of that is impossible concerning Allah. If Allah the Most Exalted were in a direction or a place, then place and direction would exist before He did whereas demonstrable proof exists that there is no priority without beginning other than Allah. Furthermore, if He were in a place

66 Sūratu 'l-Anʿam [Cattle], 6:103.
67 Sūratu 'l-Qiyāmah (The Resurrection) 75:22.
68 An aberrant, anthropomorphizing interpretation of the hadith in *Ṣaḥīḥ Muslim* (English ed. 2:616) whereby at the end of the Farewell Pilgrimage the Prophet ﷺ pointed his finger in turn at the sky then at the people, saying: "O Allah, be witness, O Allah, be witness, O Allah, be witness."

then He would need that place and this would constitute a denial of His absolute self-sufficiency.[69]

Still further, if He were in a place then He would be in it sometimes or at all times. The first alternative is false because moments in time are similar in themselves. Likewise Allah's relation to moments of time is all the same so His singling out of one of them would be a gratuitous preference of one time over another if there is no external agent who is responsible for tipping the scales; and if there is, then He would be depending on external factors to achieve spatial confinement. The second alternative is also false since from it follows the insertion of spatially confined things into places already occupied by bodies and that is absurd. Also, were it possible to point to him in a sensible fashion then he could be pointed to from every point on the surface of earth and since the earth is circular it follows that Allah is surrounded by earth from all directions. Otherwise, pointing to him would be impossible. And since He is firmly established on His throne and has taken a position on it just as the Wahhābis claim, then, his throne is surrounded by the seven heavens. Thus, it follows from His coming down to the lower level and His going up from thence, as the Wahhābis say, that His body becomes small when he goes down and gets big when he goes up. Therefore Allah would be constantly changing from one state to another!

Now the texts from the transmitted sources of Qur'an and Sunna establishing that He can be pointed to and of which the Wahhābis lay hold—these they understand superficially and they in no wise contradict certainties. They are interpreted (*tu'awwal*) either in a general sense—and the detailed meanings are left to Allah himself, just as the majority of the pious ancestors are in agreement on; or they are interpreted in a detailed fashion as according to the opinion of many, in that what is mentioned

---

[69]In *kalam* or theology Allah's "necessity" (*wujūb*) is a reference to necessary existence and self-sufficiency, which applies to Allah alone, whereas all other existence possesses only "contingency" (*imkān*).

about pointing him to the heavens is predicated upon the fact that Allah is the creator of the heavens or that the heavens are the manifestation of His power because of what they contain in the way of the great worlds in relation to which our humble world is only an atom. Likewise ascent to him is in the sense of ascent to the place to which one draws near by acts of obedience and so forth and so on with respect to Qur'anic exegesis.

## 5: How the Wahhābis Cast Aside Reason

Since clear reason and sound theory clash in every way with what the Wahhābis believe, they are forced to cast reason aside. Thus by their taking the text of Qur'an and Sunna only in their apparent meaning (*ẓāhir*) absurdity results. Indeed, this is the well-spring of their error and misguidance. For by attending only to the apparent meaning of the Qur'anic text, they believe that Allah being fixed on His throne and being high above His throne is literally true and that He literally has a face, two hands and that His coming down and His going up is a literal going down and coming up and that He may be pointed to in the sky with the fingers in a sensible manner and so forth. According to this interpretation, Allah is made into nothing less than a body. These very Wahhābis, who call visiting graves idol-worship, then, become themselves idol-worshippers by fashioning the object they worship into a body, like an animal who sits on its seat and literally comes down and goes up and literally has a hand and a foot and fingers. But the true object of worship, Allah the Exalted, transcends what they worship.

Still, if one refutes them by rational proofs and establishes that their beliefs contradict the nature of divinity by criteria recognized by reason, they answer that there is no arena for humble human minds in matters like this whose level is beyond the level of mere reason. In this respect they are exactly like Christians in their claim about the Trinity. For ask a Christian: "How is three one and one three?" they will answer: "Knowledge of the Trinity is above reason; it is impermissible to apply reasoning in this area."

There is no doubt that when reason and the transmitted text contradict each other, the transmitted text is interpreted by reason. For often it is impossible for a single judgment to affirm what each of them requires because of what is entailed by the simultaneous holding together of two contradictory propositions. Taking one side or the other, in other words, does not relieve the conflict. On the contrary, one must choose either priority of the transmitted text over reason or reason over the transmitted text. Now the first of these two alternatives has to be invalid simply because it represents the invalidation of the root by the branch.

Clearly, one can affirm the transmitted text only by virtue of reason. That is because affirmation of the Creator, knowledge of prophecy and the rest of the conditions of a transmitted text's soundness are only fulfilled by aid of reason. Thus reason is the principle behind the transmitted text on which its soundness depends. So, if the transmitted text is given precedence over reason and its legal implication established by itself aside from the exercise of reason, then the root would be invalidated by the branch. And from that the invalidation of the branch would follow as well. For the soundness of the transmitted text is derived from the judgment of reason, whose corruption is made possible when reason is invalidated.

Reason, then, is not cut off by the soundness of the transmitted text. Hence, it follows that declaring the transmitted text sound by making it prior to reason constitutes nothing less than the voiding of its soundness. But, if making something sound accomplishes its corruption, we face a contradiction: the transmitted text, then, is invalid. Therefore, if the priority of the transmitted text over reason does not exist on the basis of the preceding argument, then we have determined that reason has priority over the transmitted text. And that is what we set out to prove.

Once one realizes this, one also realizes without question the necessity of interpreting the Qur'anic verses where the apparent sense contradicts reason when the said verses are obscure and do not refer to things that are known with certainty (*yaqīnāt*). On the one hand, there is general interpretation where the detailed clarification is left to Allah (*tafwīḍ tafsīlih*). This is the school of the majority of the Pious Ancestors of our Faith (*al-Salaf*). On the other hand, we have interpretation which sets out the text's meaning in a more perspicuous fashion. The majority of later scholars (*al-khalaf*) follow the latter. In their view:

The term "to firmly establish" as in the verse of Qur'an:

﴿ ٱلرَّحْمَـٰنُ عَلَى ٱلْعَرْشِ ٱسْتَوَىٰ ﴾

*The All-Merciful is firmly established on His throne*[70]

means "He took possession of it" (*istawlā*). This is supported by the words of the poet who said: "Amr took possession (*qad istawlā*) of Iraq without bloodshed or sword."

Allah's saying: وَجَآءَ رَبُّكَ وَٱلْمَلَكُ صَفًّا صَفًّا "*And your Lord comes with angels rank on rank*"[71] means his power comes.[72]

His saying: إِلَيْهِ يَصْعَدُ ٱلْكَلِمُ ٱلطَّيِّبُ "*Unto Him good words ascend*"[73] means: good words please Him.[74] For the word is an accident for which, by itself, locomotion is impossible.

His saying:

﴿ هَلْ يَنظُرُونَ إِلاَّ أَن يَأْتِيَهُمُ اللَّهُ فِى ظُلَلٍ مِّنَ الْغَمَامِ ﴾

*Wait they for naught else than that Allah should come unto them in the shadows of the clouds with the angels?*[75]

---

[70] Sūrah ṬāḤā, 20:5.

[71] Sūratu 'l-Fajr (The Dawn) 89:22.

[72] 'His reward', as Imām Aḥmad interpreted it. See Bayḥaqī's sound report in Ibn Kathīr's *al-Bidāya wa al-Nihāya* 10:327 and Ibn al Jawzī's *Daf' Shubūb al Tashbīh* (Saqqāf ed.) p. 13.

[73] Sūratu 'l-Fāṭṭir (The Originator of Creation) 35:10.

[74] or 'His acceptance', as interpreted by Abū Ḥayyān in *Tafsīr al-Bahr al-Muḥīṭ* (7:303) and Bayḥaqī in Ibn Ḥajar's *Faṭh al-Bārī* (13:416).

[75] Sūratu 'l-Baqarah [The Heifer], 2:210.

means that His punishment should come unto them.[76]

His saying:

﴿ثُمَّ دَنَا فَتَدَلَّىٰ﴾

﴿فَكَانَ قَابَ قَوْسَيْنِ أَوْ أَدْنَىٰ﴾

*Then He drew near and came down until he was two bows' length or nearer;*[77]

means that the Prophet ﷺ came near Him by virtue of his obedience. The length of two bow-lengths is a pictorial representation in sensible fashion of what the mind understands.

In the Prophet's saying in Bukhārī and Muslim: "Allah comes down to the nearest heaven and says: who is repenting, I shall turn to him, and who seeks forgiveness, I shall forgive him" the coming down signifies Allah's Mercy.[78] He specifies night because it is the time of seclusion and various kinds of acts of humility and worship and so forth, as found in many verses of the Qur'an and narrations of the Prophet ﷺ.

## 6: Wahhābi Rejection of Consensus (*Ijma'*)

Since the very substance of the Wahhābi creed contradicts what the noble Companions, the great *Mujtahid*s and the totality of the *'Ulamā'* have reached a consensus on, they must reject Consensus as a principle (*aṣl*) of Islamic legislation and deny its probative value as a basis for practical application. In consequence, they have declared disbeliever any Muslim who says "There is no god but Allah and Muḥammad is the Messenger of Allah" other than themselves because Muslims

---

[76] Or: 'His power and His order', as Imām Aḥmad interpreted it. See Bayhaqī's sound report in Ibn Kathīr's *al-Bidāya wa-l-Nihāya,* 10:327 and *al-Jawzī fī Daf' Shubh al-Tashbīḥ* (Saqqāf ed.) p. 110 and 141.

[77] Sūratu 'n-Najm [The Star], 53:8-9.

[78] As reported also from some of the Salaf, such Imām Mālik: see Ibn 'Abd al-Barr, *al-Tamḥīd* (7:143) and al-Dhahābī's *Siyar A'lām al-Nubalā'* (8:105).

visit the graves of prophets and *awlīyā*, and ask Allah for something for the sake of a prophet.

They pronounce this declaration of unbelief despite the fact that the Muslim Community has reached a consensus that whoever articulates the twofold testimony of faith or *shahāda*, the ordinances of the religion become immediately binding. As we have seen from the hadith: "I have been ordered to fight people until they say: 'There is no god but Allah,'" and the hadith: "It is sufficient that folk say: 'There is no god but Allah.'" Ibn Qayyim has said: "Muslims have reached a consensus that when the disbeliever says: 'There is no god but Allah and Muḥammad is the Messenger of Allah, he enters Islam.'" For that reason, there is a general agreement that when the apostate apostatizes by an act of idolatry, repentance is accomplished by utterance of the *shahāda*.

Furthermore, Wahhābis consider seeking the intercession of the Prophet ﷺ after his death an act of disbelief (*kufr*) even though a consensus allowing it is in place. At the same time, they say following and emulating the legal rulings of one of the four *Mujtahid*s, Imam Abū Hanifa, Imam Shafi'i, Imam Malik and Imam Aḥmad Ibn Ḥanbal is prohibited. As a result, anyone, they say, may derive legal rulings (*istinbāṭ al-aḥkām*) directly from the Qur'an according to their capability; notwithstanding the existence of consensus to the effect that no one is capable of being an Imam in the religion or school of law unless he satisfies the criteria for a scholar capable of legal reasoning (*Mujtahid*). It is not up to anyone to take from Qur'an and Sunna until he has satisfied those criteria by joining in himself the qualifications of the *Mujtahid* which are, simultaneously, the conditions of *ijtihād*.

*Ijtihād* is the agreement of the *Mujtahid*s of the Muslim community in a certain generation on a matter of religion or dogma. A corollary to this is that consensus on any matter is absent after the disappearance of a generation of *Mujtahid*s. While this is the case, one knows that if no consensus has been agreed upon, there exists a possibility in each generation of reaching a settlement on questions about which a clear ruling in Qur'an and Sunna is absent and which *Mujtahid*s of the past have not discussed.

Consider these examples. A man hears it said that the earth is moving around the sun. Without thinking, he says: "If the earth is moving around the sun, then my wife is divorced," since there is no clear evidence in Qur'an and Sunna for affirming the earth's movement around the sun. The *'Ulamā'* of the Muslim community therefore need to make a clear pronouncement regarding this question. Hence, their consensus regarding the earth's motion does not exist until a question like this is settled.

Or, suppose a man fasts, riding in a balloon in the air before the setting of the sun and he is lifted into the air until he arrived at the height of ten thousand miles. Then the sun sets on earth and the people on land break their fast but the sun is not absent from his eyes when he is in the air by reason of the earth's roundness. Is it permitted for him to break fast and it is obligatory for him to pray Ṣalāt al-Maghrib? This is an example where there is no clear ruling upon in Qur'an and Sunna. It follows, then, that the *'Ulamā'* of a generation must clarify a judgment of things like this and agree upon it. And what we say agrees with Imam Ghazali's definition of *ijma'*. He defines it as agreement of the community of Muḥammad ﷺ upon a certain matter and what is meant by agreement is the manifest and unhidden agreement of its *'Ulamā'*.

Those that deny *ijma'* claim: the occurrence of such a consensus is impossible. They deduce evidence for their denial by arguing that agreement of the *'Ulamā'* presupposes their being equally placed with regard to the legal situation in question. Their being scattered in remote countries over the face of the earth precludes this. We refute this objection by rejecting the reasoning that the *'Ulamā'*'s being spread abroad is an impediment to their agreement in view of the (unconditional) strictness of their scrutiny of Shari'a evidences.

Those rejecting *ijma'* claim further that agreement is based either on an indication (*dalīl*) in the sources which is decisive (*qaṭ'i*) or on a speculative one (*ẓannī*). Both, they say, are invalid. The decisive indication is invalid because, they say, if it were existent there would be no need for recourse to agreement in the first place; and the speculative indication is invalid because agreement on a ruling is impossible since temperaments differ and points of view differ out of natural habit. Our answer is a rejection of both their objections. Regarding the decisive indication there is no need of transmitting it since consensus is stronger than it, and for the elimination of difference entailed through its transmission. With regard to the speculative indication, their objection does not stand up because of the possibility of consensus being too obvious for either differences of temperament and/or point of view to prevent it. Only in what is minute and obscure lie impediments to reaching consensus.

In further objection, they claim: Even if we grant establishment of consensus in itself, then knowledge of their agreement would still be impossible. They argue that in the habitual course of things there is no chance of affirmation of a legal ruling concerning this thing or the other declared by every individual member of the *'Ulamā'* in the world. Likewise, they argue that in the habitual course of things transmission of a consensus is impossible because its transmission from single individuals is not conveyed and the consensus does not issue in practical application. One simply cannot conceive of a thing being so widely known that lying about it is impossible (*tawātur*)—they claim—inasmuch as such a situation would involve the necessary equaling out of points of view on a given state of affairs with the result that pro and con positions and a middle position would be unfeasible. Moreover, it is unlikely that people informed of something so well-known that lying about it is impossible to have seen and heard all the *'Ulamā'* in every country and in that fashion to have transmitted it from them, generation to generation, until it reaches us.

To both their arguments there is one answer. Its procedure consists in causing one to doubt that there exists a conflict with what is necessary. For it is well known in a decisive manner that the Companions and the Successors reached a consensus on the priority of a decisive indication over a speculative one and that this is the case only by reason of its being established with them and its transmission to us. Furthermore, *ijma*ʿ constitutes a proof in the view of all the *ʿUlamā*ʾ except the Mu'tazilite al-Nazzam and some of the Khawārij. The proof of its evidentiary nature (*ḥujjiyyah*) is that they agree upon the decisive certainty of the error of contradicting *ijma*ʿ. *Ijma*ʿ therefore counts as proof in Shariʿa legislation because custom transforms the agreement of a number of many recognized *ʿUlamā*ʾ from the status of non-decisive to the status of decisive certainty in a matter pertaining to the Shariʿa. By virtue of custom the implication of a decisive text necessarily counts as decisive indication that to contradict *ijma*ʿ is error.

On this point, no one says here that there is affirmation of *ijma*ʿ by *ijma*ʿ nor affirmation of *ijma*ʿ by a decisive text whose establishment is itself dependent on *ijma*ʿ: that would be to reason in a circle. We are saying: what is being claimed is that the fact of *ijma*ʿ itself constitutes a proof for *ijma*ʿ. What establishes this is the existence of a decisive text indicated by the existence of a formal consensus, which custom precludes were it not for that text. The establishment of this formal consensus and its customary indications pointing to the existence of a text are not dependent upon the fact that *ijma*ʿ constitutes a proof. This is because the existence of such formal consensus is derived from *tawātur*—what is known as true beyond doubt so that the possibility of people's collusion on a lie is precluded—and because the formal evidence indicating a text is derived from the custom.

Among the evidences for the probative value of *ijma*ʿ is the Prophet's statement, on him be peace:

"My community will never agree on error (*al-khaṭā'*)."

The content of this hadith is so well-known that it is impossible to lie about it (*mutawātir*)[79] simply because it is produced in so many narrations, for example:

> "My community will not come together on a mis-guidance";[80]
>
> "A group of my community will continue in truth until the dawning of the Hour";[81]
>
> "The hand of Allah is with the congregation (*al-jama'a*)";[82]
>
> "Whoever leaves the community or separates himself from it by the length of a span, dies the death of the *Jāhilīyah* (period of ignorance prior to Islam)";[83]

---

[79] Ghazālī has pointed out that this hadith is not *mutawātir*... Having said this, however, al- Ghazālī adds [*Mustaṣfā* 1:111] that a number of prominent Companions have reported *aḥādīth* from the Prophet ﷺ, which although different on their wording, are all in consonance on the theme of the infallibility of the community and its immunity from error... [Both he and *al-Āmidī* in *al-Iḥkām fī uṣūl al-aḥkām* 1:220-221] observe that the main purport of these *aḥādīth* ...convey positive [*qaṭī*] knowledge, and that the infallibility of the *ummah* is sustained by their collective weight." Mohammad Hashim Kamali, *Principles of Islamic Jurisprudence* (Cambridge: Islamic Texts Society, 1991) p. 178. See Ibn al-'Arabi al-Maliki's list of the *aḥādīth* pertaining to *ijma'* in his commentary on Tirmidhī's relevant section in Kitāb al-Fitan: *'Āriḍat al-Aḥawdhī by Ibn al-'Arabī al-Mālikī* (Beirut: Dār al-Kutub al-'Ilmiyyah, n.d.), vol. 9, pp. 8–11

[80] Ibn Mājah 2:1303 #3950.

[81] *Mutawātir* (Bukhārī and Muslim).

[82] Tirmidhī (*hasan*).

[83] Muslim (Kitāb al-Imārah #55) through Ibn 'Abbās. Muslim relates it with slight variations through three more chains. Ibn Abī Shayba also relates it in his *Muṣannaf*.

and so forth. As for the solitary hadiths (*āḥad*) involved, even if they are not widely attested, they possess value equivalent to the widely attested hadith and, indeed, positive knowledge results from them just like stories we hear relating the courage of Imam ʿAlī and the generosity of Ḥātim.

The deniers of the evidentiary nature of *ijmaʿ* use as proof the verse from the Qur'an:

﴿ وَنَزَّلْنَا عَلَيْكَ ٱلْكِتَٰبَ تِبْيَٰنًا لِّكُلِّ شَىْءٍ ﴾

*And We reveal the Scripture unto thee as an exposition of all things.*[84]

Then they say that there is no reference for the exposition of legal rulings except the Qur'an. The answer to them is this does not preclude that there can be something other than the Book also exposing matters; nor does it preclude that the Book can expose certain things by means of the *ijmaʿ*. If it did, we would wind up with external meanings which nevertheless do not oppose the decisive texts.[85]

They also invoke against the probative nature of *ijmaʿ* Allah's statement:

﴿ فَإِن تَنَٰزَعْتُمْ فِى شَىْءٍ فَرُدُّوهُ إِلَى ٱللَّهِ وَٱلرَّسُولِ ﴾

*If you differ in anything among yourselves, refer it to Allah and His Messenger.*[86]

Therefore there is no source of reference, they claim, other than Qur'an and Sunna. The answer is: this text refers specifically to what people are "differing about." But what is agreed upon is not like that. Or it specifically concerns the Companions. If we

[84] Sūratu 'n-Nahl [The Bee], 16:89.
[85] *al-ẓāhir lā yuqawwimu al-qāṭiʿ*: "The external sense does not stand in opposition to what is decisively known."
[86] Sūratu 'n-Nisā [Women], 4:59.

were to accept that this is not the case, then, again, one ends up with external meanings not clashing with what is decisive just as we claimed earlier.

In addition, they adduced the hadith of Muʿadh as evidence that he left out *ijmaʿ* when he mentioned his evidences in answer to the Prophet's query about them, and the Prophet ﷺ approved what he said.[87] They say this indicates that *ijmaʿ* does not count as evidence. The answer is Muʿadh did not mention it only because at that time *ijmaʿ* did not yet constitute a formal proof in case of failing to settle upon a source with respect to Qur'an and Sunna. It does not follow that *ijmaʿ* did not become a proof in its own good time and after taking its place as a source.

## 7: The Wahhābis Denial of the Principle of Analogy (*Qiyās*)

Wahhābis reject analogy (*qiyās*) in legal reasoning just as they reject consensus. By rejecting it, however, they only intend to discredit the authority of those truly capable of independent reasoning in deriving legal rulings in the Muslim Community, that is, the *Mujtahids* of the four recognized schools of Islamic law. The Wahhābis allege that the *Mujtahid*s cast aside the Qur'an and Sunna and operate only on the basis of their personal opinions to the point of criticizing the Imams of the Umma for using qiyās as a proof in Shariʿa. They denounce by saying that the Imams believe that the religion of Islam is deficient and that

[87]It is reported that the Prophet ﷺ asked Muʿadh ibn Jabal upon the latter's departure as judge to the Yemen: "How will you apply judgment when the occasion arises?" He said: "I shall judge according to Allah's Book." The Prophet ﷺ asked: "And if you do not find [an answer]?" He said: "Then by the Sunna of His Messenger." The Prophet ﷺ said: "And if you do not find [an answer]?" He said: "Then I shall do my best to form an opinion and spare no pain." The Prophet ﷺ slapped his chest and said: "Praise belongs to Allah Who has blessed the messenger of Allah's Messenger's with something pleasing to Allah's Messenger." Related by Abū Dāwūd (Eng. 3:1019 #3585).

they complete it by reasoning like of *ijma*ʿ and qiyās. For this, they cite the Qur'anic verse:

﴿ ٱلْيَوْمَ أَكْمَلْتُ لَكُمْ دِينَكُمْ ﴾

*This day I have perfected for you your religion.*[88]

They say we find whatever is necessary for life clearly stated in the Qur'an. So what need do we have for qiyās. The texts take in the whole of life's eventualities, they claim, without need of derivation (*istinbāṭ*) and analogy.

It is amazing that the Wahhābis, for the sake of calumny against *Mujtahid*s who accept *qiyās* themselves, proceed to toy with the word of Allah and verses of Qur'an and manipulate them, changing them from their correct meaning and interpreting them according to their own passion and whim. And yet they have no interpretation of the superficial sense of the verses of the Qur'an that does not disparage the Creator—in keeping with their literalism according to which Allah is established firmly on His throne and has hands and a face. They say that the *Mujtahid*s operate according to their own opinions, even though they go so far as to allow the ignorant riffraff of those possessing their faith to comment upon the Word of Allah according to their own limited understanding.

*Qiyās* is the equating of the branch with the root with respect to the cause of the legal ruling. Its essential elements are four:

1) the original root which is the object of comparison;
2) the branch or subsidiary case being likened to root;
3) the ruling governing the root;
4) the general attribute which is the aspect under which the comparison is being made.

The legal ruling of the new case is not an essential element of it since it is the fruit of the analogy and its consequence. An

[88] Sūrat al-Mā'idah [The Spread Table], 5:3.

example of analogy is when we say a drink made of fermented figs is an intoxicant, then it is forbidden by analogy to wine by the evidence of the statement: "Wine is prohibited":[89]

1) The original case is wine, that is, the object of comparison.
2) The new case which is like it is the drink made from fermented figs which is what is being compared to the wine.
3) The legal ruling in the original case is prohibition.
4) The general attribute is intoxication.

Analogy counts as a proof because the Companions had acted by it repeatedly despite the silence of the others. In a case like that the silence is the agreement of custom because of Qur'anic command: فَاعْتَبِرُوا *fa'tabirū—"Consider and reflect!"*[90]. It is well known that "consideration" consists of making an analogy of one thing to another which is not an exception.

Even if this did not constitute an argument, many matters would remain that we see come into existence in the course of time whose legal status is overlooked, and regarding whose status the criteria for judging are absent from the apparent meaning of the texts in the Qur'an and Sunna. Yet this does not contradict Allah's statement:

﴿وَلَا حَبَّةٍ فِي ظُلُمَاتِ الْأَرْضِ وَلَا رَطْبٍ وَلَا يَابِسٍ إِلَّا فِي كِتَابٍ مُّبِينٍ﴾

*There is not a grain in the darkness or depths of the earth, nor anything fresh or dry but is inscribed in a clear Record.*[91]

What is meant by "clear Record" here is the Preserved Tablet on which Allah has deposited what was and what will be.

---

[89] Anas and others in Bukhārī and Muslim.
[90] Sūrat al-Ḥashr, 59:2.
[91] Sūrat al-An'ām, 6:59.

We may say that since the root of the analogy is mentioned with its legal ruling in the Book, the branch to which the root's ruling is applied is considered mentioned as well, for it is built upon the root. Or again we say: It is obvious that the manner in which the content of the Book of Allah embraces every green and dry is not all explicit. Rather, many of the legal rulings of Qur'an come into being by pure derivation (*istinbāṭan*). And among the modes of derivation there is *qiyās*. So the Wahhābis' statement whereby the texts of Qur'an and hadith pertain to all of life's phenomena without derivation or analogy is not granted. Their containing all of life's phenomena is only complete by their application.

## 8: Their Denial of *Taqlīd* and of the *Ijtihād* of Past Sunni Scholars

Since the statements of the *Mujtahids* of the past—may Allah have mercy upon them—and the established religious rulings to which they have arrived clash with what the deviant sect of Wahhābis have devised in the way of unwarranted innovation, that sect deemed it a necessity to deny the validity of their *Ijtihād*, reject the soundness of their opinions, and declare whoever followed their opinions to be an unbeliever. The result of this is that they have the freedom of action to establish themselves far and wide and to scream and play with the religion just as their passions dictate. Thus, they pave the way for founding the basis of their clear misguidance. For if they did not deny the *Ijtihād* of the *Mujtahid*s of the past, then their application, in accordance with their whim, of the verses of the Qur'an revealed concerning idolaters to Muslims and to those who make their petitions to Allah for the sake of the honor of His Messenger and respect of the saints (*awlīyā*) could not have been brought to pass. That is because they focus on what no *Mujtahid* said in the first place and what none of Imams of the Religion accepted.

All of this misguidance is due to the unwarranted innovator Ibn ʿAbd al-Wahhāb who displayed marked resemblance to those who claimed prophethood like Musaylima and Abū al-Aswad al-

Anasī and other liars. For he was concealing in himself the establishment of a religion which imitated the pattern of those liars. But he feared to show people his lies unlike they who showed their lies. What he made appear to people he put in the guise of support of the Islamic faith while he painted this picture in people's minds that he simply wanted pure monotheism and that people had become idolaters. Thus, the jihad with people followed so that they might "return from their idolatry." Therefore, Ibn ʿAbd al-Wahhāb claimed absolute *Ijtihād* for himself and charged with error whoever preceded him belonging to the *Mujtahids*—those great figures who dipped from the sea of knowledge of the Prophet ﷺ—and declared disbeliever their followers. He did not permit imitating the opinions of anyone other than himself, although he allowed anyone his of his ignorant followers to interpret the Qur'an in whatever mode their limited understanding gave them access, and to derive legal rulings from them on the basis of their weak grasp of its meaning. It was as though he permitted any one of his followers to be a *Mujtahid*. Look at the way he played with religion and toyed with the Shariʿa of the Faithful Messenger of Allah!

As for his claim of absolute *Ijtihād*, it is pure silliness on his part and shameless impudence with regard to the Arab language since he was not in his time one of those recognized for being foremost in knowledge. On the contrary, he was not even numbered among those who were considered by masters in the Hanbali madhhab as having any weight whatsoever, not to mention being considered an absolute *Mujtahid* in the religion.

*Ijtihād* has conditions which the *ʿUlamāʾ* have agreed upon without exception and it is not permissible for any individual to be an imam in the religion and in any of the schools of Islamic Law, unless he has fulfilled them.

## Conditions of *Ijtihād*

1) He must be a master of the language of the Arabs, knowing its different dialects, the import of their poems, their proverbs, and their customs.[92]

2) He must have a complete grasp of the differing opinions of the scholars and jurists of Islam.[93]

3) He must be a jurist himself, learned in the Qur'an, having memorized it and knowing the difference of the seven readings of the Qur'an while understanding its commentary, being aware of what is clear and what is obscure in it, what it abrogates and what is abrogated by it, and the stories of the prophets.

4) He must be learned in the Sunna of the Messenger of Allah, capable of distinguishing between its sound hadith and its weak hadith, its continuous hadith and hadith whose chain of transmission is broken, its chains of transmission, as well as those hadith which are well known.[94]

5) He must be scrupulously pious in the religion, restraining his lower desires with respect to righteousness and trustworthiness, and his doctrine must be built upon the Qur'an and the Sunna of the

---

[92]It is not necessary, according to consensus, that he possess profound erudition in the Arabic language (*tabahhur*), but it is enough that he have a moderate erudition (*tawassuṭ*) as described by Zahawī.

[93]By this are meant the science of differences of opinions (*ʿal-khilāf*), the science of consensus in opinions (*ʿilm al-ijmaʿ*), and the science of analogy and its kinds (*ʿilm(ʿilm al-qiyās*).

[94]It is not necessary that he reach the rank of hadith master (*ḥāfiẓ*), as Suyūṭī in *al-Radd ʿalā man akhlada* points out by listing non-*ḥāfiẓ* absolute *mujtahids* (*mujtahid muṭlaq*) such as Abū Isḥāq al-Shīrāzī, Ibn al-Ṣabbāgh, al-Juwaynī, and al-Ghazālī.[94]It is not necessary that he reach the rank of hadith master (*ḥāfiẓ*), as al-Suyūṭī in *al-Radd ʿalā man akhlada* points out by listing non-*ḥāfiẓ* absolute *mujtahids* (*mujtahid muṭlaq*) such as Abū Isḥāq al-Shīrāzī, Ibn al-Ṣabbāgh, al-Juwaynī, and al-Ghazālī.

> Prophet ﷺ. One who is missing in any of these characteristics falls short and is not permitted to be a *Mujtahid* whom people imitate.[95]

Ibn al-Qayyim in *I'lām al-Muwaqqi'īn* does not permit anyone to make derivation from the Qur'an and Sunna as long as he has not fulfilled the conditions of *Ijtihād* with respect to the Islamic sciences. A man asked Aḥmad ibn Ḥanbal: "If a person memorized a hundred thousand hadiths, is he a jurist (*faqih*)?" Imam Aḥmad said: "No." He said: "Two hundred thousand hadiths?" Imam Aḥmad said: "No." Three hundred thousand hadiths? Again, he said: "No." "Four hundred thousand hadiths?" Finally, he said: "Yes."[96] It is said that Aḥmad Ibn Ḥanbal gave legal answers on the basis of six hundred thousand hadith.[97]

Know that people have agreed generation after generation and century after century that the *Mujtahid* Imams only derive legal rulings from the Qur'an and the Sunna after they have completely studied the Sunna and its sciences and the Qur'an with respect to its rulings and understanding, in a way unmatched by those who followed them in later times. On the contrary, the *'Ulamā'*, generation after generation, take hold of what they said, scholars of the caliber of al-Nawawī, al-Rāfi'ī, Taqī al-Dīn al-Subkī, Ibn

---

[95] Al-Suyūṭī has listed among the mujtahids whose mastery is recognized simultaneously in the three disciplines—jurisprudence, ḥadīth, and the Arabic language: himself, Ibn al-Ṣalāḥ, Abū Shāmah, al-Nawawī, Ibn Daqīq al-'Īd, and Taqī al-Dīn al-Subkī, among others.

[96] Al-Sakhāwī relates in the introduction to his biography of Ibn Ḥajar al-'Asqalānī, entitled *al-Jawāhir wa al-Durar*, that Aḥmad said neither yes nor no to the figure of 300,000, but he gestured with his hand that it was acceptable (Cairo, 1986 ed., p. 26). Ibn al-Jawzī relates in *al-Ḥathth 'alā ḥifẓ al-'ilm* (Alexandria ed., 1983, p. 43) that Abū Zur'ah said that Imām Aḥmad knew no less than 1,000,000 ḥadīths.

[97] According to Imām Aḥmad's statement reported by al-Ḥākim in his *Madkhal li- 'Ulūm al-Ḥadīth* (Robson ed., p. 13), there were 7,000,000 sound ḥadīths known in his time, of which the ḥāfiẓ Abū Zur'ah had memorized six; and he sat at Bukhārī's feet like a young boy learning. All these numbers refer to chains of transmission, not texts.

Ḥazm, Ibn Taymiyya, Ibn al-Qayyim, Ibn al-Jawzī, scholars like Fakhr al-Dīn al-Rāzī, al-Ṭaḥāwī, al-Qāsim, al-Qarāfī: all were imitating the opinions of the *Mujtahid*s and their followers, despite the fact that each one of these leading figures and those before them had delved deep into every category of the Islamic sciences. Yet and still, they knew that they had not arrived at the level of deriving law from Qur'an and Sunna independently. What's more, they understood their own limits. May Allah have mercy on the man who knows his measure and does not go beyond his proper level.

So how is it possible for any one of us from this later time to derive law from Qur'an and Sunna and to cast aside the *ʿUlamā'* who were capable of deriving law and whom both the elite and the masses of the Muslims agree on following?

Ibn ʿAbd al-Wahhāb's labeling disbeliever those who imitate the opinion of the Mujtahids of the past, as mentioned previously is only to initiate spread of his unwarranted innovation (*bidʿa*) in our faith so that he may only considers Muslim those who follow him. Would that I knew what would happen if we supposed that past Mujtahids had gone astray, as Ibn ʿAbd al-Wahhāb has claimed, and they had, indeed, gone astray. Would it be incumbent upon the common person to practice Islam while being unable to know how to derive legal rulings from Qur'an and Sunna with Ibn ʿAbd al-Wahhāb having not yet been born to resolve the difficulty of their confusion and ignorance? I do not believe that he would have arrived at the temerity to say those people were living in the primordial state of natural religion (*fiṭra*) since they came in a time prior to a "renewer of religion"![98]

---

[98]These are the renewers of religion according to Ahl al-Sunna:
1st Century: ʿ Umar ibn ʿAbd al-ʿAzīz (62-101)
2nd: - Abū Ḥanīfah (80–150), Mālik (93–179), al-Shāfiʿī (150–204)
3rd Century: Aḥmad ibn Ḥanbal (164–241), Abū al-Ḥasan al-Ashʿarī (260–324)
4th Century: al-Ḥākim al-Naysābūrī (321–405)
5th Century: al-Bayhaqī (384–458), al-Ghazālī (450–505)

The present writer knows that following an authority in matter of Islamic practice (*al-taqlīd*) is necessary inasmuch as, ordinarily speaking, it is impossible that each individual Muslim reach the level of knowledge enabling him to derive legal rulings of the Shariʿa directly from Qur'an when there is no plain meaning text and he is completely ignorant of the Arabic language like non-Arab people such as Persians, Kurd, Afghans, Turks, and others whose number increases beyond the number of Arabs, a fact obvious to any one with a knowledge of geography. The scholars of Islam have agreed that it is incumbent upon a person who has not reached the stage of *Ijtihād* to follow and imitate the legal rulings of a *Mujtahid.* For Allah has said:

﴿فَاسْأَلُواْ أَهْلَ الذِّكْرِ إِن كُنتُمْ لاَ تَعْلَمُونَ﴾

*Ask those who have knowledge* (*Ahl al-dhikr*) *if you do not know.*[99]

And the Prophet ﷺ said: "Did they ask when they did not know? For the only remedy of incapacity in such instances is to ask a question."[100]

---

6th Century: Fakhr al-Dīn al-Rāzī (544–606)
7th Century: al-Nawawī (631–676), Ibn Daqīq al-ʿĪd (d. ~702)
8th Century: Taqī al-Dīn al-Subkī (683–756), al-Bulqīnī (724–805)
9th Century: al-ʿAsqalānī (773–852), al-Suyūṭī (849–911)
10th Century: al-Shaʿrānī (898–973)
11th Century: al-Fārūqī al-Sirhindī (971–1034)
12th Century: Ibn ʿAlawī al-Ḥaddād (1046–1132)
13th Century: Khālid al-Baghdādī (1193–1242)
14th Century: al-Kawtharī (d. 1371)

[99]Sūrat al-Naḥl, 16:43.

[100]Related by Abū Dāwūd.
Ibn Qayyim said: "There is an obligatory (*wājib*) *taqlīd*, a forbidden *taqlīd*, and a permitted *taqlīd*... The obligatory *taqlīd* is the *taqlīd* of those who know better than us, as when a person has not obtained knowledge of an evidence from the Qur'an or the Sunna concerning something. Such a *taqlīd* has been reported from Imām al-Shafiʿi in many places, where he would say: "I said this in *taqlīd* of ʿUmar" or "I said that in *taqlīd* of ʿUthman" or "I said that in *taqlīd* of ʿAta'." As Al-Shafiʿi said concerning the Companions—may Allah be well

## 9: Their Naming Muslims Disbelievers (*Takfīr*)

Wahhābis have pretexts for their doctrine to in order to construct a foundation for their unwarranted innovation in religion. One of them is to declare Muslims unbelievers. That is because Ibn ʿAbd al-Wahhāb, as you know by now, has been seduced by the evil promptings of his ego into attempting to create a new religion by which he could obtain political leadership. However, when he saw that this could not be brought to pass in the land of Muslims—for, in spite of their extreme ignorance, they held fast to the faith of Islam—he created the innovation in Islam itself. Furthermore, when he saw that the matter could not be accomplished except after declaring Muslims disbelievers by using some semblance of Qur'anic evidence, he found that the only way to declare them unbelievers was through their calling on Allah by using their Prophet as a means (*tawassul*) as well as for the sakes of other prophets, *awlīyā* and pious persons. Likewise he levelled the same charge at those who vow or perform sacrifices for their sakes and perform other acts whose description I shall bring later. All these matters he considers worship of the prophets and the saints. And since the Qur'an is jam-packed with clearly articulated verses to the effect that one who worships something or someone other than Allah, he is an idolater, Ibn ʿAbd al-Wahhāb makes all monotheists idolaters because of the state of affairs just described.

Since the Wahhābis have declared disbeliever all Muslims who differ with them, they have made their country the land of warfare (*bilād ḥarb*). Then they have made licit the shedding their blood and seizing their property. Yet Allah, the Exalted, has said:

﴿إِنَّ ٱلدِّينَ عِندَ ٱللَّهِ ٱلْإِسْلَٰمُ﴾

---

pleased with all of them: "Their opinion for us is better than our opinion to ourselves." Ibn Qayyim, *Aʿlam al-muwaqqiʿīn ʿan rabb al-ʿalamīn* 2:186-187.

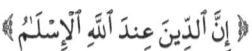

*Surely, religion with Allah is the Surrender* (*al-Islam*).[101]

And the Prophet ﷺ has said: "Islam consists in testifying that there is no god but Allah and that Muḥammad is the Messenger of Allah." Also, in the hadith of Ibn ʿUmar we find: " Islam is built upon five things: Testifying that there is no god but Allah and that Muḥammad is the His servant and Messenger," to the end of the hadith. There is the hadith of the delegation of ʿAbd al-Qays: "I order you to believe in Allah alone. Do you know what belief in Allah alone is? It is to bear witness that there is no god but Allah and that Muḥammad is the Messenger of Allah."[102] Ibn Qayyim said: "All Muslims agree that if the disbeliever says: 'There is no god but Allah and Muḥammad is the Messenger of Allah,' he enters Islam."

Know that to declare a Muslim a unbeliever is no small matter. The *ʿUlamāʾ*, among them Ibn Taymiyya and Ibn Qayyim,[103] have agreed that the ignorant person and the one who makes a mistake in this community, even if what is done makes its perpetrator an idolater or disbeliever, and that person pleads the excuse of ignorance or that he made a mistake until a proof is explained to him in a lucid and clear fashion, a situation like such a person's is ambiguous.[104] The Muslim might have joined in him disbelief, idolatry and faith. Yet he does not disbelieve in such a way that carries him out of the religion.

## 10: Apostasies and Heresies

The Khawārij were the first to separate from the Congregation of Muslims. The Messenger of Allah had spoken about them and ordered them to be killed and fought: "They will pass through Islam like an arrow passes through its quarry. Wherever you

---

[101] Sūrat Āli ʿImrān [the Family of ʿImrān], 3:19.

[102] All three are related by Bukhārī and Muslim.

[103] Zahāwī mentions them often because Salafis consider them their highest scholarly authorities. Yet, as he shows, they contradict them on many foundational issues, such as this one.

[104] I.e. he cannot be declared an unbeliever.

meet them, kill them!"[105] "They are the dogs of the people in Hell."[106] "They recite Qur'an and consider it in their favor but it is against them."[107] The Khawārij went out of Islam in the time of our master 'Alī, may Allah be pleased with him. They declared him and Mu'awiya disbelievers and declared licit their blood and property as well as the blood and property of those with him. They made the land of the former a land of war and declared their own land an abode of faith. They only accepted from the Prophet's ﷺ Sunna what agreed with their own doctrine, deduced evidence for their doctrine from what was not perspicuous in the Qur'an, and applied the verses revealed concerning the idolaters to the people of Islam. Yet despite their disbelief, neither the Companions nor the Successors declared them disbelievers, just as Ibn Taymiyya has transmitted. 'Alī said to them: "We do not start out killing you nor are you kept out of the mosques of Allah in which you mention His name. We do not rescind the rights of protection with respect to your life and property afforded you by Islam as long as your hand is with us." The great among the Companions debated the Khawārij, like Ibn 'Abbās, until four thousand returned to the truth.

As for the fighting of the people of the *Ridda*—apostates—one category among them apostatized Islam and returned to the disbelief which they were on with respect to idol worship. Another category apostatized and followed Musaylima and they were the Banū Ḥanīfah and some other tribes. Yet another group apostatized, followed and agreed with al-Aswad al-'Ansīyy, in Yemen. Others said claims of Ṭulayḥah al-Asadīyy were true; they were the Ghaṭafān, Fazāra and other tribes. Still others did the same with respect to Sujah. All these denied the Prophethood of Muḥammad, may Allah bless him and grant him peace. They

---

[105]Bukhārī and Muslim have more than one form of this hadith.
[106]Sound (*ṣaḥīḥ*) hadith related through various chains by Ibn Mājah, Muqaddima 12, and Aḥmad 4:355, 382, 5:250, 253, 256, 269.
[107]These and many other *aḥādīth* have been understood by some scholars to apply to the Wahhabis as well. See above, section following the bibliography.

refused to pay the tax on Muslims and to pray, abandoning the rest of the Shariʿa as well. One class of apostates distinguished between prayer and the tax. They denied the obligatoriness of conveying the latter to the Imam. In reality, those are the People of Rebellion (*baghī*). The name "*Ridda*" was attached to them only because of their entry into the throng of the apostates.

The Qadariyya separated from the Congregation of Muslims in the final period of the time of the Companions. They were composed of two sects. The first directly denied the divine Decree (*qadar*). They said that Allah did not foreordain His servants to commit acts of disobedience nor does he guide the one in error and foreordain the guidance. In their view, the Muslim is one who makes himself Muslim by himself and the one who prays makes himself a prayer by himself, and so forth and so on with respect to other acts of obedience and disobedience. This sect makes the servant the creator (*khāliq*) of his own deeds instead of Allah.

The second sect is just the opposite of the first. They claim that Allah compels people to act in a certain way and that disbelief and disobedience among human creatures are like the black and white color of their skins. In their view, the creature has no part to play in doing none of this. On the contrary, all acts of disobedience in their view are ascribable to Allah. The perpetrators of such acts are the followers of Iblis where he says:

﴿ قَالَ فَبِمَآ أَغْوَيْتَنِى لَأَقْعُدَنَّ لَهُمْ ﴾

*Because You have sent me astray, I shall ambush them*[108].

Similarly, the idolaters say:

﴿ لَوْ شَاءَ اللَّهُ مَا أَشْرَكْنَا وَلَا آبَاؤُنَا ﴾

---

[108] Sūrat al-Aʿrāf, 7:16.

*Had Allah willed, we nor our forefathers would not have been idolaters.*[109]

Yet for all this disbelief and misguidance on the part of the Qadariyya, not one of the Companions nor any of the Successors declared them to be disbelievers. Rather, they stood right before them and explained to them their misguidance from the Qur'an and Sunna. They did not make killing them an obligation incumbent on Muslims nor exact against them the judgments made against the people of apostasy.

Then, the Mu'tazila separated from the Congregation of Muslims in the period of the Successors. Among their doctrines of disbelief is their claim that the Qur'an is created. They also deny that the Prophet ﷺ, can intercede in the behalf of perpetrators of acts of disobedience and assert that perpetrators of disobedience will reside eternally in hell fire and so on and so forth with respect to their teachings. Again, not one of the *'Ulamā'* of that time declared them unbelievers but the scholars among the Successors and those who succeeded them confronted them. They refuted them and explained to them the falsity of their doctrine. They did not exact on them the laws against apostates. On the contrary, on them and those before who made unwarranted innovations in the religion they carried out the Muslim laws of inheritance and marriage and buried them in Muslim ground.

Then there was the Murji'a who claimed that faith (*īmān*) resided in the verbal assertion of belief and not in the deed. Hence, in their view, one who articulates the twofold declaration bearing witness to his faith is a believer even if he does not perform a single act of prayer the whole of his life, nor fast one day of Ramadan. Yet despite their lingering in error and their continual dogged resistance to change even after the people of truth explained to them the error of their school of thought, no one

---

109 Sūrat al-An'ām [The Cattle], 6:148.

declared them unbelievers. Rather, they treated them and the people of unwarranted innovation before them as brethren of fixed and stable faith.

The Jahmiyya separated from the Congregation of Muslims. They said no Allah who is an object of worship is upon the throne nor does Allah have any speech as on earth. They denied Allah the attributes that He affirms of Himself in His clear Book and which His true and faithful Messenger affirms of Him and all the Companions. Likewise, they denied the vision of Allah in the hereafter and so forth and so on with respect to their doctrines of disbelief. In spite of that, the *'Ulamā'* refuted them and demonstrated to them their misguidance until they killed some of their propagandists like Jahm Ibn Ṣafwān and al-Ju'd Ibn Dirham. But after killing them they ritually cleansed their bodies, prayed for them and buried them in Muslim ground. They did not carry out the rulings for people guilty of apostasy.

Then the Rāfiḍah or "Rejecters" separated from the Congregation of Muslims. They agreed with the Mu'tazila in their belief that they were the sole creators of their own actions. They denied the vision of the Creator on the Day of Judgment. They declared most of the Companions to be unbelievers and they vilified the Mother of the Believers ('A'isha). Despite all this non of the '*'Ulamā'* declared them to be unbelievers nor did they forbid the rulings of inheritance and marriage apply to them; rather they applied to them the same rulings that applied with all Muslims.

Those following the school of thought of the Pious Ancestors—which the Wahhābis attempt to hide behind—are distinguished by the signal absence of declaring deviant groups unbelievers as we have mentioned. Shaykh Taqī al-Dīn Ibn Taymiyya said that Imam Aḥmad did not declare the Khawārij disbeliever, nor the Murji'a nor the Qadariyya nor the individuals of the Jahmiyya. Indeed, he prayed behind the Jahmiyya who called people to their doctrine while they punished harshly those who did not agree with them. Ibn Taymiyya also said in essence that among the blameworthy innovations is declaring a group among the

Muslims to be unbelievers, making their blood and wealth licit because of rejected innovations. For, he said, there may be in that group less unwarranted innovation than in the party carrying out the declaration of disbelief. Even if one supposes a group to have made unwarranted innovation, it is unwarranted for the group which is on the path of the Sunna to declare them unbelievers, since, perhaps, its innovation is an outgrowth of an error, and Allah said:

﴿رَبَّنَا لَا تُؤَاخِذْنَا إِن نَّسِينَا أَوْ أَخْطَأْنَا﴾

*Our Lord do not blame us if we forget or make a mistake*[110]

and:

﴿وَلَيْسَ عَلَيْكُمْ جُنَاحٌ فِيمَا أَخْطَأْتُم بِهِ وَلَكِن مَّا تَعَمَّدَتْ قُلُوبُكُمْ﴾

*The mistake you make will not be held against you but what your hearts on purpose intend.*[111]

The Prophet ﷺ said: "Surely, has Allah forgiven my community error and forgetfulness and what they were forced to do."[112]

The Consensus has long since concluded that whoever confirms what the Messenger has brought—even if there be in it some trace of disbelief and idolatry—should not be declared a unbeliever until the proof is furnished. The only proof that can be furnished is in the strength of Consensus not speculative but decisive. Further, the one who furnishes the proof is the Leader of the Muslims or his deputy. But disbelief only exists when one denies things necessary to the religion of Islam such as the existence of the Creator and his unity, the rejection of the message of Muḥammad or the rejection of the duties of Islam like the obligatoriness of prayer.

---

110 Sūratu 'l-Baqarah [The Heifer], 2:286.
111 Sūrat al-Aḥzāb [The Confederates], 33:5.
112 Ibn Mājah, Talaq 16. Ṭabarānī also relates it through two good chains. See Haythami, *Majmaʿ al-zawa'id.*

The school (*madhhab*) of the People of the Prophet's Way and the Congregation of Muslims (*Ahl al-Sunnah wa al-Jamāʿah*) shrinks from declaring anyone belonging to the religion of Islam an unbeliever. This holds even to the point of suspending pronouncements of disbelief against people who introduce unwarranted innovations into Islam, despite the command to kill them out of defense against the harms they may do—not because of their disbelief. For there may be found joined in a single individual disbelief (*kufr*), belief (*īmān*), hypocrisy (*nifāq*), and idolatry (*shirk*) and he is not a complete disbeliever. Whoever confesses Islam it is accepted from him whether he be truthful or lying. Even if signs of hypocrisy and ignorance are manifest on him, he is excused from disbelief. The same is true of hesitation and doubt even if this be weak. By now the unwarranted innovation on the part of the Wahhābis should be manifest in any case, when they introduce an unwarranted innovation by declaring Muslims disbelievers and thereby contradict what Allah has brought to us in the Qur'an and by the Sunna of His Messenger ﷺ as well as the statements of the Imams of the religion and the learned *Mujtahids*.

## The Wahhābis' Rejection of *Tawassul* (Using a Means)

In the preceding sections we have spoken about the way the Wahhābis declare any Muslim a disbeliever for contradicting their unwarranted innovations in our religion, and the way they ascribe to that person idolatry. The moment has now come to speak of how they take, as a pretext for their declaration of disbelief, the seeking of help from the prophets and *awlīyā* and their use of the latter as a means to Allah and the visiting of their graves. For the Wahhābis have rejected these practices and claimed they are forbidden (*ḥarām*).

## Their Hatred of Muslims Who Make *Tawassul*

The Wahhābis have made their rejection of those seeking aid (*mustaghīthīn*), those using persons as means of access to Allah (*mutawassilīn*), and those visiting graves (*zā'irīn*), especially intense. They consider them actual idolaters and idol-worshippers. Indeed, they deem their status worse than the idolaters of old. The latter, they say, were idolaters only with respect to divinity. As for the Muslim idolaters—they mean those who contradict them— they have associated a partner both to divinity and to lordship. They also say that the unbelievers in the time of the Messenger of Allah did not always practice idolatry but they sometimes practiced polytheism and sometimes practiced monotheism, abandoning calling on prophets and men of righteousness. That is because when times were good they prayed to them and believed in them. But when disaster and difficulties struck, they abandoned them, worshipped Allah faithfully and sincerely, and recognized that the Prophet ﷺs and pious could do them neither good nor ill.

## Their Assimilation of Muslims to Idol-Worshippers by Quoting the Qur'an

The Wahhābis applied the Qur'anic verses revealed concerning the idolaters to the monotheists of the Community of Muḥammad, Allah's blessings and peace be upon him, and grasped on to these verses as a basis for declaring Muslims disbeliever. They may be listed as follows:

﴿فَلَا تَدْعُوا مَعَ اللَّهِ أَحَدًا﴾

*Do not call on anyone along with Allah*[113]

﴿وَمَنْ أَضَلُّ مِمَّن يَدْعُو مِن دُونِ اللَّهِ مَن لَّا يَسْتَجِيبُ لَهُ إِلَى يَوْمِ الْقِيَامَةِ وَهُمْ عَن دُعَائِهِمْ
غَافِلُونَ وَإِذَا حُشِرَ النَّاسُ كَانُوا لَهُمْ أَعْدَاء وَكَانُوا بِعِبَادَتِهِمْ كَافِرِينَ﴾

*And who is more astray than one who invokes besides Allah such as will not answer him to the day of judgment and when mankind are gathered they will become enemies for them, and deny having been worshipped.*[114]

---

[113] Sūrat al-Jinn [The Jinn],72:18.
[114] Sūrat al-Aḥqāf [The Wind-Curved Sandhills], 46:5-6.

﴿وَلَا تَدْعُ مِن دُونِ ٱللَّهِ مَا لَا يَنفَعُكَ وَلَا يَضُرُّكَ فَإِن فَعَلْتَ فَإِنَّكَ إِذًا مِّنَ ٱلظَّٰلِمِينَ﴾

*Nor call on any other than Allah such as can neither profit you nor hurt you: if* you *do, behold! You shall certainly be of those who do wrong.*[115]

﴿وَالَّذِينَ تَدْعُونَ مِن دُونِهِ مَا يَمْلِكُونَ مِن قِطْمِيرٍ﴾

﴿إِن تَدْعُوهُمْ لا يَسْمَعُوا دُعَاءَكُمْ وَلَوْ سَمِعُوا مَا اسْتَجَابُوا لَكُمْ وَيَوْمَ الْقِيَامَةِ يَكْفُرُونَ

بِشِرْكِكُمْ وَلا يُنَبِّئُكَ مِثْلُ خَبِيرٍ﴾

*And those whom you invoke besides Him own not a straw. If ye invoke them, they* will *not listen to your call, and if they were to listen, they cannot answer your prayer. On the day of Judgment they will reject your partnership and none, O Man! can inform you like Him who is All-aware.*[116]

﴿فَلا تَدْعُ مَعَ اللَّهِ إِلَهًا آخَرَ فَتَكُونَ مِنَ الْمُعَذَّبِينَ﴾

*So call not on any other god with Allah, or thou will be among those who will be punished;*[117]

﴿لَهُ دَعْوَةُ الْحَقِّ وَالَّذِينَ يَدْعُونَ مِن دُونِهِ لاَ يَسْتَجِيبُونَ لَهُم بِشَيْءٍ إِلاَّ كَبَاسِطِ كَفَّيْهِ إِلَى

الْمَاء لِيَبْلُغَ فَاهُ وَمَا هُوَ بِبَالِغِهِ وَمَا دُعَاء الْكَافِرِينَ إِلاَّ فِي ضَلالٍ﴾

*To Him is due true prayer; any others that they call upon besides Him hear them no more than if they were to stretch forth their hands for water to reach their mouths but it reaches them not. For the prayer of those without faith is vain prayer.*[118]

---

115 Sūrat Yūnus, [Jonah], 10:106.
116 Sūrat al-Fāṭir [The Originator ], 35:13-14.
117 Sūrat al-Shuʿarāʾ [The Poets], 26: 213.
118 Sūrat al-Raʿd [The Thunder], 13:14.

﴿ أُوْلَٰئِكَ الَّذِينَ يَدْعُونَ يَبْتَغُونَ إِلَىٰ رَبِّهِمُ الْوَسِيلَةَ أَيُّهُمْ أَقْرَبُ وَيَرْجُونَ رَحْمَتَهُ وَيَخَافُونَ
عَذَابَهُ إِنَّ عَذَابَ رَبِّكَ كَانَ مَحْذُورًا ﴾

*Say: Call on those besides Him whom ye fancy; they have no power to remove your trouble from you or to change them. Those unto whom they cry seek for themselves the means of approach to their Lord, which of them shall be the nearest; they hope for His mercy and fear His wrath: for the wrath of thy Lord is something to take heed of.*[119]

These and other verses have been revealed with respect to the idolaters among the Arabs. Ibn ʿAbd al-Wahhāb, however, claims that whoever seeks help by the Prophet ﷺ, implores or calls upon Allah by means of the Prophet ﷺ of someone else among the prophets, *awlīyā* or pious, or asks for the Prophet's intercession or visits his grave is considered in the class of idolaters contained within the scope of the above verses. His specious argument concerning these verses is based on the idea that though they were revealed concerning the idolaters their admonition belongs to the general sense of the expression and not the specificity of the cause.

## Refutation of This Falsehood

We do not deny that the admonition belongs to the general sense of the expression and not with a specific cause. However, we say that these verses do not refer to the people whom the Wahhābis claim they embrace since the Muslims who make *tawassul* (using means) and *istighātha* (seeking aid) in no way share the state of the unbelievers concerning whom the verses were revealed. Invocation (*duʿā*) comes in a variety of senses which we will soon mention. However, in all these verses it has the sense of worship, and Muslims only worship Allah the Exalted; none of them ever adopted prophets and *awlīyā* as gods,

---

[119] Sūrat al-Isrā' [The Night Journey],17:57.

making them partners with Allah so that the general sense of these verses would apply to them. Muslims do not believe that prophets and *awlīyā* are entitled to worship since they have not created anything nor do they have control over harm and benefit. On the contrary, they believe that they are Allah's servants created by Him. By visiting their graves and imploring Allah in their name they only intend being blessed by means of their blessing for they are alive, near to Allah and He has selected and chosen them. Hence, he shows mercy to His servants by means of their blessing and heavenly benediction (*baraka*).

## Further False Comparison of Muslims to Idolaters

The Wahhābis say: the defense of those who practice *tawassul* is the same apology the idolaters of the Arabs offered as the Qur'an says describing the way the idolaters defended their worship of idols:

﴿ مَا نَعْبُدُهُمْ إِلاَّ لِيُقَرِّبُونَا إِلَى اللَّهِ زُلْفَى ﴾

*We only worship them in order that they may bring us nearer.*[120]

Hence, the idolaters do not believe that the idols create anything. Rather, they believe that the Creator is Allah, the Exalted, by evidence of the following verse:

﴿ وَلَئِن سَأَلْتَهُم مَّنْ خَلَقَهُمْ لَيَقُولُنَّ اللَّهُ فَأَنَّى يُؤْفَكُونَ ﴾

*If thou ask them, Who created them, they will certainly say, Allah*[121]

and:

﴿ وَلَئِن سَأَلْتَهُم مَّنْ خَلَقَ السَّمَاوَاتِ وَالأَرْضَ لَيَقُولُنَّ اللَّهُ ﴾

[120] Sūrat al-Zumar, [The Groups], 39:3.
[121] Sūrat al-Zukhruf [Ornaments of Gold], 43:87.

*If indeed thou ask them who is that created the heavens and the earth, they would be sure to say, Allah.*[122]

Allah has only judged against them for their disbelief because they say "*We only worship them in order that they may bring us nearer.*" The Wahhābis say: Thus, do people who implore Allah by prophets and the pious use the phrase of the idolaters: "In order to bring us nearer" in the same sense.

## Refutation of That False Comparison

The answer contains several points:

- The idolaters of the Arabs make idols gods; while the Muslims only believe in one Allah. In their view, prophets are prophets: *awlīyā* are *awlīyā* only. They do not adopt them as gods like the idolaters.
- The idolaters believe these gods deserve worship contrary to what Muslims believe. Muslims do not believe that anyone by whom they implore Allah deserve the least amount of worship. The only one entitled to worship in their view is Allah alone, May He be Exalted.
- The idolaters actually worship these gods as Allah relates: "*We only worship them...*" Muslims do not worship prophets and pious persons by the act of imploring Allah by means of them.
- The idolaters intend by their worship of their idols to draw near Allah just as He relates concerning them. As for the Muslims, they do not intend by imploring Allah by means of prophets and saints to draw close to Allah, which is only by worship. For that reason, Allah said in relating about the idolaters: "... in order that they bring us nearer." However, Muslims only intend blessings (*tabarruk*) and intercession (*shafa'a*) by them. Being blessed by a thing is obviously different from drawing near to Allah by it.

---

[122] Sūrat al-Zumar, [The Groups], 39:38.

Since the idolaters believe that Allah is a body in the sky, they mean by "*to bring us near*" a literal bringing near. What indicates this is its being stressed by their use of the word *zulfā*—nearness to power—inasmuch as emphasizing something by its own same meaning indicates for the most part that what is intended by it is the literal meaning and not the metaphorical. For when we say: "He slew him murderously" (*qatalahu qatlan*) a literal killing rushes to the understanding, not that of "a hard blow" in counter distinction to what we mean when we just say: "He slew him"; for that might mean only a hard blow. The Muslims do not believe that Allah is a body in the sky remote enough from them to see a literal proximity to Him by imploring Allah through a prophet. The ruling of Shari'a contained in the verse does not apply to them, whereas since the Wahhābis believe that Allah is a body who sits on his throne, they do not discover a meaning of blessing which the Muslims intend by their imploring Allah by prophets and *awlīyā*, but only that of drawing near which belongs to bodies. For that reason, these verse are applicable to them not to Ahl al-Sunna.

## Kinds of *Shirk*

We ought here to explain the various forms of idolatry or association of partners with Allah or *shirk*. First, we find the *shirk* of making-independent, such as affirming two independent gods like the *shirk* of the Zoroastrians. Secondly, there is the *shirk* of dividing into parts, that is, making-compound but of a number of gods like the *shirk* of the Christians. Thirdly, there is the *shirk* of drawing-near, that is, the worship of something other than Allah in order to draw near to Allah in a closer fashion. This is exemplified in the *shirk* of the Period of Ignorance prior to Islam.

The kind of *shirk* that Wahhābis made applicable to the Muslim making *istighātha* and *tawassul* and upon which Wahhābis built their doctrine of calling Muslims disbelievers belongs to the third category, the *shirk* of drawing-near which the *Jāhiliyya* professed as its religion.

The state of affairs that delivered the *Jāhiliyya* into its form of idolatry is a type of satanic seduction whereby its worship of Allah in its idolatrous manner stemmed from extreme human weakness and powerlessness; and a belief that not to draw near to Him by worshipping those nearest to Him, nobler in His sight, and more powerful, like the angels, would constitute bad manners. But when they observed the disappearance of the objects of their worship either constantly or some of the time they fashioned idols to represent them; so that when the objects of worship disappeared from them, they worshipped their images.

If this is firmly understood, then it is clear to the reader that the state of the idolaters of the *Jāhiliyya* does not in any way apply to Muslims imploring Allah by the means of prophets and the pious. The Arabs of the *Jāhiliyya* adopted idols as gods. "Allah" means "One who deserves worship." They believed the idols deserved worship. First of all, they believed that they could deliver harm and benefit. Thus, they worshipped them. This belief on their part plus their worship of them is what caused them to fall into idolatry. So when the proof was furnished them that these idols had no power to harm them or benefit them, they said: "*We only worship in order that they bring us nearer.*" How, then, is it possible for the Wahhābis to assimilate the believers who declare that Allah is One to those idolaters of the *Jāhiliyya*?

There is no doubt that Arab idolaters disbelieved simply because of their worship of statues and representations of prophets, angels, and *awlīyā* of which they formed images which they worshipped and to which they did sacrifice. This was due to their belief that prophets, angels, and *awlīyā* are gods (*āliha*) along with The Allah (*allah*) and could, on their own, do them benefit and harm. The Allah therefore furnished proof of the falsity of what they were saying and struck parables to refute their doctrine which He did in many verses. These verses state that the one Allah who alone is entitled to worship necessarily has power over removing harm and delivering benefit to him who worships Him; and that what they in fact worshipped were objects originating in time and antithetical to Lordship. Persons who seek help and who call upon Allah by means of prophets are free and innocent of this order of idolatrous worship and belief.

As for the claim that seeking aid (*istighātha*) is worship of someone other than Allah, it is high-handed and arbitrary. For the verses which the Wahhābis adduce as proof-texts—all of them—were revealed to apply to unbelievers who worship someone other than Allah. They intended by their worship of that other individual to come closer to Him. Furthermore, they believed that there is another god along with Allah and that He has a son and a wife—exalted exceedingly high is He beyond what they say. This is a point of unanimous agreement which no one disputes. There is nothing in the verses revealed concerning the unbelievers that would count as evidence that merely seeking the help of a prophet or saint when accompanied by faith in Allah is worship of someone other than Allah Himself.

## Refutation of Their Claim that *Tawassul* Is Worship of Other than Allah

The Wahhābis say that such seeking of help is a form of invocation. They cite the hadith:

*Inna al-du'ā' huwa al-'ibāda*: "Invocation—it is worship."[123] Hence, they claim, he who asks help from a prophet or a saint (*walī*) is simply worshipping him by that request for help; yet only worship of Allah alone is beneficial and worship of other than Him is *shirk*. Hence, they conclude, the one who seeks aid of someone other than Him is an idolater.

The answer for this is that the verbal pronoun *huwa* ("it is") in the hadith conveys restriction of the grammatical predicate

---

[123]Aḥmad 4:267, 271, 276; Tirmidhī, Tafsīr of 2:16 (#2969) and 40 (#3247, #3372) (*ḥasan ṣaḥīḥ*); Abū Dāwūd "Kitāb al-Witr" # 1479 (*ṣaḥīḥ*); Ibn Ḥibbān; Bukhārī in *al-Adab al-mufrad* (*ṣaḥīḥ*); Ibn Mājah, "Kitāb al-Du'ā" Ch. 1 (#3828), and Bayhaqī in Shu'ab al-'Īmān 2:37 (#1105bis); without "*inna*": Muslim, al-Ṭabarānī, al-Ḥākim, al-Nasā'ī, and Ibn Abī Shaybah.

"worship" to its subject "invocation" and it thus renders definite the predicate, just as the author of *al-Miftāḥ*[124] says and with whom the majority of the scholars agree concerning this hadith. Thus, for example, when we say: إِنَّ ٱللَّهَ هُوَ ٱلرَّزَّاقُ "*Allah—He is the Provider*" (*Allāh huwa al-Razzāq*)[125], it means there is no provider other than He. Accordingly, when the Prophet ﷺ said: "Invocation: it is worship" he signified that worship is restricted to invocation. What is meant by the hadith is:

"Worship is nothing other than invocation."

And the Qur'an supports this meaning when it says:

﴿قُلْ مَا يَعْبَأُ بِكُمْ رَبِّى لَوْلَا دُعَآؤُكُمْ﴾

*Say: My Lord would not concern Himself with you but for your call* (*duʿā*) *on Him.*[126]

That is, He would not have shown favor to you were it not for your worship. For the honor of mankind lies in its worship and its respect in its knowledge and obedience. Otherwise, man would not be superior to the beasts. The Hajj, the Zakat, the Fast and the Testimony of Faith are all invocation and likewise reading of the Qur'an, *dhikr* or remembrance, and obedience. Hence, worship is confined to invocation. Once this is firmly established, it becomes clear that there no is proof in the hadith for what Wahhābis claim, because if asking for help is a kind of invocation, as the Wahhābis claim, it does not necessarily follow that asking for help is worship, since invocation is not always worship as is plain to see.[127]

If, on the contrary, we restrict the subject "invocation" to the predicate "worship" in the hadith according to the interpretation

---

[124]Suyūṭī: *Miftāḥ al-Jannah fī al-Iʿtiṣām bi-l-Sunnah.*
[125]Sūrat al-Dhāriyāt [The Winnowing Winds], 51:58.
[126] Sūrat al-Furqān [The Criterion], 25:77.
[127]E.g. in the sense of calling someone.

of the author of *al-Kashshāf*[128] whereby the definition of the predicate in a nominal clause might be either restricted to the subject or restricted to the predicate, then the logical deduction of the Wahhābis whereby all *du'ā* is worship is still not supported by it. Otherwise, the definite article *al* in *al-du'ā* (invocation or literally a call on someone) makes invocation generic and betokens universal inclusion into the genus. Yet this is not the case since not every invocation is an act of worship (*'ibāda*).

On the contrary, the matter stands as we find it in the verse of Qur'an:

﴿وَلَا تَدْعُ مِن دُونِ ٱللَّهِ مَا لَا يَنفَعُكَ وَلَا يَضُرُّكَ﴾

*Nor call on other than Allah such as can neither profit thee nor hurt thee*[129] and similarly in the verse:

﴿وَٱدْعُوا۟ شُهَدَآءَكُم﴾

*Call your witnesses or helpers!.*[130] Calling on Allah in the sense of requesting is found where the Qur'an says:

﴿ ٱدْعُونِىٓ أَسْتَجِبْ لَكُمْ﴾

*Call on Me and I will answer you*[131] and in the sense of a declarative statement:

﴿ دَعْوَاهُمْ فِيهَا سُبْحَانَكَ اللَّهُمَّ﴾

*This will be their prayer* (*da'wāhum*) *therein: Glory to Thee, O Allah!*[132]

---

[128]al-Zamakhsharī's Qur'anic commentary entitled *al-Kashshāf 'an ḥaqā'iq al-tanzīl wa-'uyūn al-aqāwīl fī wujūh al-ta'wīl.*

[129] Sūrah Yūnus [Jonah],10:106.

[130] Sūratu 'l-Baqarah [The Heifer], 2:23.

[131] Sūrah Ghāfir [The All-Forgiving], 40:60.

[132] Sūrah Yūnus [Jonah],10:10.

As for "calling on someone" in the sense of summoning them (*nidā'*), we find:

﴿ يَوْمَ يَدْعُوكُمْ ﴾

*It will be on the day when he will call you* (*yad'ūkum*)[133] and in the sense of naming someone we find:

﴿ لا تَجْعَلُوا دُعَاءَ الرَّسُولِ بَيْنَكُمْ كَدُعَاءِ بَعْضِكُم بَعْضًا ﴾

*Deem not the calling* (*du'ā*) *of the Messenger of Allah among yourselves like the calling of one of you to another.*[134]

As the author of *al-Itqān*[135] makes plain: If the definite article belongs to the genus and signifies universal inclusion therein, then the man who says: "Zayd! Give me a dirham" perpetrates an act of disbelief. Yet the Wahhābis, of course, will not claim this. Hence, it is plain that the definite article signifies specification. So what is meant by invocation in the hadith is *invocation to Allah* and not calling on someone in the general sense. The meaning would be:

> "Calling to Allah is one of the greatest acts of worship."
>
> It is in the manner of the Prophet's saying: "*al-ḥajju 'arafatun*" or:
>
> "The Pilgrimage is 'Arafah"[136]

which is taken to mean that this represents the Hajj's greatest essential element. For the one making the request comes toward

---

[133] Sūrat al-Isrā' [The Night Journey],17:52.
[134] Sūrat al-Nūr , [The Light], 24:63.
[135] Suyūṭī: *al-Itqān fī 'Ulūm al-Qur'ān.*
[136] Tirmidhī, Tafsīr 2:22; Abū Dāwūd, Manāsik 68; Ibn Mājah, Manāsik 57; Dārimī, Manāsik 54.

Allah and turns aside from what is other than He. Furthermore, the request is commanded by Allah and the action fulfilling that command is worship. The Prophet ﷺ names it "worship" to show the subjugation of the subject making the request, the indigence of his condition, and the humility and lowliness of his worship.

Among the proofs that what is meant by "invocation" in the hadith is the "calling on Allah" and not the general sense of "calling" is the fact which many grammarians confirm and Ibn Rushd clearly makes plain as does al-Qarafī also in his Commentary on *al-Tanqīḥ*:[137] namely, that asking (*al-su'āl*) is one of the categories of wanting (*al-ṭalab*) put forth by one lower to one higher in station. If it is addressed to Allah, it is named "request" (*su'āl*) and "invocation" (*du'ā*). The latter is not applied to someone other than Allah. And if it is not permissible (*lā yajūz*) to name the request of other than Allah by the unqualified name of *du'ā*, then such a request *a fortiori* is not named a *du'ā* in the sense of worship.

## 11: *Tawassul* (Using means): Evidence for its Permissibility

Before plunging into this chapter let us clarify one thing pertaining to what one means by seeking help with the Prophet ﷺs and pious persons and imploring Allah by means of them. First, they are means and causes to obtain what is intended. Second, Allah is the true agent of the favor or miracle which comes at their hand, not they themselves, just as true doctrine asserts in the case of other actions: for the knife does not cut by itself but the cutter is Allah the Exalted, although the agent is the knife in the domain of the customary connection of events. Be that as it may, it is Allah who creates the cutting.

Al-Subkī, al-Qasṭallānī in *al-Mawāhib al-Laduniyya*, al-Samhūdī in *Tārīkh al-Madīna*, and al-Haythamī in *al-Jawhar al-*

[137] *Sharḥ Tanqīḥ al-Fuṣūl fī al-Uṣūl* by Aḥmad ibn Idrīs al-Qarāfī al-Mālikī (d. 1285 CE).

*Munaẓẓam* said that seeking help with the Prophet ﷺ and other prophets and pious persons, is only a means of imploring Allah for the sake of their dignity and honor (*bi jāhihim*). The one doing the asking seeks from the One asked that He assign him aid (*ghawth*) on behalf of the one higher than him. For the one being asked in reality is Allah. The Prophet ﷺ is but the intermediary means (*wāsiṭa*) between the one asking for help and the One asked in reality. Hence, the help is strictly from Him in its creation (*khalqan*) and being (*ījādan*), while the help from the Prophet ﷺ is strictly in respect to secondary causation (*tasabbuban*) and acquisition from Allah (*kasban*).

The most prominent among the scholars of Islam have acknowledged the permissibility of *istighātha* and *tawassul* with the Prophet ﷺ, peace be upon him.[138] Its permissibility is not contravened by the report of Abū Bakr, may Allah be pleased

---

[138]Imām Aḥmad, for example. 'Alā' al-Dīn al-Mardāwī said in his book *al-Inṣāf fī Ma'rifat al-Rājiḥ min al-Khilāf 'alā Madhhab al-Imām al-Mubajjal Aḥmad ibn Ḥanbal* (3:456): "The correct position of the [Hanbali] *madhhab* is that it is permissible in one's supplication (*du'ā'*) to use as means a pious person, and it is said that it is desirable (*mustaḥabb*). Imām Aḥmad said to al-Marwadhī: *yatawassalu bi-al-nabī fī du'ā'ihi*—Let him use the Prophet ﷺ as a means in his supplication to Allah.'"
al-Ḥāfiẓ Taqī al-Dīn al-Subkī said: "Verily Allah knows that every goodness in my life which He has bestowed upon me is on account of the Prophet ﷺ that my recourse is to him, and that my reliance is upon him in seeking a means to Allah in every matter of mine. Verily he is my means to Allah in this world and the next." In *Fatāwa al-Subkī,* beginning of the article entitled "The Descent of Tranquility and Peace on the Nightlights of Madina" (*Tanazzul al-Sakīna 'alā Qanādīl al-Madīna*) 1:274.
Imām Shawkānī said in his commentary on al-Jazarī's (d. 833) '*Iddat al-Ḥiṣn al-Ḥaṣīn* entitled *Tuhfat al-Dhākirīn bi-'Uddat al-Ḥiṣn al-Ḥaṣīn*: "He [al-Jazarī] said: Let him make *tawassul* to Allah with His Prophets and the *ṣāliḥīn* or saints (in his *du'ā'*). I say: And exemplifying *tawassul* with the Prophets is the hadith extracted by Tirmidhī *et al.* (of the blind man saying: O Allah, I ask You and turn to You by means of Muhammad the Prophet of Mercy)... as for *tawassul* with the saints, among its examples is the hadith, established as sound, of the Companions' *tawassul* asking Allah for rain by means of al-'Abbās the Prophet's ﷺ uncle, and 'Umar said: "O Allah, we use as means to You the uncle of our Prophet etc." (Beirut ed. 1970) p. 37.

with him, whereby when he said "Rise! [plural], We will seek help with the Messenger of Allah from this hypocrite," the Prophet ﷺ said:

> *'innahu lā yustaghāthu bihi, 'innamā yustaghāthu bi-llāh*
>
> "Help is not sought with me, it is sought only with Allah."

Since Ibn Luḥay'a is part of its chain of transmission, the discussion of it is well-known.[139]

Were we to suppose that the hadith is sound, it would be of the like of the Qur'anic verse,

﴿وَمَا رَمَيْتَ إِذْ رَمَيْتَ وَلَٰكِنَّ اللَّهَ رَمَىٰ﴾

*You did not throw when you threw, but Allah threw*[140] and the Prophet ﷺ said, "I did not bear you but Allah bore you."[141] Thus the meaning of the hadith "Help is not sought with me" is:

> "(Even if I am the one ostensibly being asked for help,) I am not the one being asked for help, in reality Allah Himself is being asked."

In sum, the term *istighātha* or "asking for help" applies to whomever the help comes from including in respect to causation and acquisition;[142] this is what the Arabic means and the Shari'a permits. The hadith "Help is not sought with me" must be interpreted in the light of this. This meaning is supported by the

---

[139]Suyūṭī, *Jāmi' al-Aḥādīth*, 496 #2694. Haythami in *Majma' al-Zawā'id*: "Ṭabarānī related it and its men are those of sound hadith except Ibn Luḥay'a who is fair (*ḥasan*)."

[140]Sūrat al-Anfāl [The Spoils of War], 8:17 and: "*Those who swear allegiance unto thee swear allegiance only unto Allah*" Sūrat al-Fatḥ [The Victory], 48:10.

[141]Bukhārī and Muslim.

[142]I.e. secondary causes.

hadith in *Ṣaḥīḥ al-Bukhārī*[143] touching on intercession on the Day of Resurrection. Such was the help people sought from Adam, then Ibrāhīm, then Mūsā, then ʿIsā, then Muḥammad, on him and them be Allah's blessings and peace.

Now we have come to the point of setting forth the permissibility of *tawassul* and adducing evidence for it. We find in the Qur'an:

﴿ يَا أَيُّهَا الَّذِينَ آمَنُواْ اتَّقُواْ اللّهَ وَابْتَغُواْ إِلَيهِ الْوَسِيلَةَ ﴾

*O ye who believe! Be wary of Allah and seek al-wasīlah—the means to approach Him.*[144]

Ibn ʿAbbās said that *al-wasīlah* signifies whatever means one employs to draw close to Allah. The Wahhābis claim that "means" refers exclusively to actions and this is pure arbitrariness. The manifest and apparent sense (*ẓāhir*) of the text refers to persons (*dhawāt*) not actions. For Allah says: *ittaqū Allāh* (Fear Allah) which conveys the sense of wariness in doing whatever Allah has ordered and relinquishing whatever He has forbidden. If we interpret "seek the means" in terms of actions, then the order of "seeking the means" would consist in an emphasis (*ta'kīd*) of the command: "Be wary of Allah." This is different than if "seeking the means" is interpreted to refer to persons. For then the command of *taqwā* is to actually lay a basis (*ta'sīs*) for one's action and this is better than emphasis.[145]

Again, Allah says:

﴿ أُوْلَئِكَ الَّذِينَ يَدْعُونَ يَبْتَغُونَ إِلَى رَبِّهِمُ الْوَسِيلَةَ أَيُّهُمْ أَقْرَبُ ﴾

---

[143] *Kitāb al-Tawḥīd.*

[144] Sūrat al-Mā'idah [The Table Spread], 5:35.

[145] To be wary of Allah is itself a means to Him, therefore the order that follows it ("Seek a means to Him"), if it refers to actions, is a reiteration of the action already named ("Fear Allah") for emphasis. This Zahāwī calls *ta'kīd*. If it refers to persons, however, it is a definition of a distinct action rather than a reiteration of the action already named. This Zahāwī calls *ta'sīs*. In the latter case the strength of the two orders is greater.

*Those unto whom they cry seek for themselves the means of approach to their Lord, which of them shall be the nearest.*[146]

Ibn ʿAbbās said they are Jesus عليه السلام and his mother, Azrael عليه السلام and the angels. And the commentary on this verse is that the unbelievers worship prophets and angels because they regard them as their lords. Thus Allah says to them, "Those whom you worship are imploring Allah by who is nearer. How, then, do you make them lords when they are servants in need of their Lord and imploring Him by One who is higher in rank than they are?"

Allah also said:

﴿وَمَا أَرْسَلْنَا مِن رَّسُولٍ إِلاَّ لِيُطَاعَ بِإِذْنِ اللَّهِ وَلَوْ أَنَّهُمْ إِذ ظَّلَمُواْ أَنفُسَهُمْ جَاؤُوكَ فَاسْتَغْفَرُواْ اللَّهَ وَاسْتَغْفَرَ لَهُمُ الرَّسُولُ لَوَجَدُواْ اللَّهَ تَوَّابًا رَّحِيمًا﴾

*If they had only, when they were unjust to themselves, come unto thee and asked Allah's forgiveness, and then the Messenger had asked forgiveness for them, they would have found Allah indeed Oft-returning, Most Merciful.*[147]

Allah has linked their seeking of forgiveness from Him with seeking forgiveness from the Prophet ﷺ. So in this verse from the Qur'an we have clear evidence of imploring Allah by means of the Prophet ﷺ and acceptance of the one that implores Him in this fashion. We understand this also from the statement: "*They would have found Allah Oft-returning, Most Merciful.*"

Asking forgiveness for his community, you should know, is not tied to his being alive and the hadiths cited shortly indicate this. One cannot say that the verses cited among a definite group of people have no general applicability; for even if they are cited among a definite group while the Prophet ﷺ was alive, they maintain a general relevance by the generality of the cause

---

[146] Sūrat al-Isrā' [The Night Journey], 17:57.

[147] Sūratu 'n-Nisā [Women], 4:64.

occasioning their utterance. So the verses take in whomever satisfies such a description whether he be alive or dead.[148]
Another evidence is the Qur'anic verse:

﴿فَاسْتَغَاثَهُ الَّذِى مِن شِيعَتِهِ عَلَى الَّذِى مِنْ عَدُوِّهِ﴾

*Now the man of his own people appealed to him [Mūsā] against his foe.*[149]

Here Allah attributes a request for help to a creature who is asking someone other than Himself. This is sufficient evidence for the permissibility for asking someone other than Allah for help.

If someone objects and says that the help being sought in these texts is from someone alive and who has power over his actions, the reply is that attributing the power to him if it is held to issue

---

[148]Al-ʿUtbī said: As I was sitting by the grave of the Prophet ﷺ, a Beduin Arab came and said: "Peace be upon you, O Messenger of Allah! I have heard Allah saying: "*If they had only, when they were unjust to themselves, come unto thee and asked Allah's forgiveness, and the Messenger had asked forgiveness for them, they would have found Allah indeed Oft-returning, Most Merciful*" Ibid., so I have come to you asking forgiveness (of Allah) for my sin, seeking your intercession with my Lord." Then he began to recite poetry:

*O best of those whose bones are buried in the deep earth,*
*And from whose fragrance the depth and height have become sweet,*
*May I be the ransom for a grave which thou inhabit,*
*And in which are found purity and bounty and munificence!*

Then he left, and I dozed and saw the Prophet ﷺ in my sleep. He said to me: "O ʿUtbī, run after the Bedouin and give him glad tidings that Allah has forgiven him."

Related in: al-Nawawī, *al-Adhkār*, Mecca ed., pp. 253–254; *al-Īḍāḥ fī manāsik al-ḥajj*, chapter on visiting the Prophet ﷺ; Ibn Ḥajar al-Haythamī, *al-Jawhar al-munaẓẓam* [commentary on al-Nawawī's *Īḍāḥ*]; al-Qurṭubī, commentary on Q 4:64 in *Aḥkām al-Qur'ān* 5:265; al-Samhūdī, *Khulāṣat al-Wafā'*, p. 121 (from al-Nawawī); al-Dahlān, *Khulāṣat al-Kalām* 2:247; Ibn Kathīr, *Tafsīr* 4:64 and *al-Bidāyah wa-al-Nihāyah* 1:180; Abū Muḥammad ibn Qudāmah, *al-Mughnī* 3:556; Abū al-Faraj ibn Qudāmah, *al-Sharḥ al-Kabīr* 3:495; al-Bahūtī al-Ḥanbalī, *Kashshāf al-Qināʿ* 5:30; Taqī al-Dīn al-Subkī, *Shifā' al-Siqām*, p. 52; and Ibn al-Jawzī, *Muthīr al-Gharām al-Sākīn ilā Ashraf al-Amākin*.

[149]Sūrat al-Qaṣaṣ [The Stories], 28:15.

from him in a fashion independent of Divine assistance is the same as *kufr*, that is disbelief. And if it is only Allah's power to be a cause and means, then there is no difference between living and dead. Thus the recipient, alive or dead, possesses the miracle as a token of respect and honor. If the seeking of aid is not related to Allah literally and to someone else figuratively, the seeking of help is forbidden in either case. From this you know the secret of the Prophet's formal rejection of seeking help from himself when Abū Bakr al-Ṣiddīq ﷺ said: "Rise! We will ask the Messenger of Allah for help from this hypocrite" and the Messenger of Allah said to him: "Help is not sought from me. Help is sought from Allah" despite the fact that the Prophet ﷺ was then alive and had power over his actions. He only intended to deny the seeking of help from him literally and in reality. For he wanted to teach his Community that help only can be sought, in reality, from Allah.

We find another evidence for *tawassul* in the Qur'anic verse:

﴿ لا يَمْلِكُونَ الشَّفَاعَةَ إِلاَّ مَنِ اتَّخَذَ عِندَ الرَّحْمَنِ عَهْدًا﴾

*They do not possess intercession save those who have made a covenant with their Lord.*[150]

Some of the commentators on Qur'an say that the "covenant" (*al-ʿahd*) is the phrase: "There is no god but Allah and Muḥammad is the Messenger of Allah." The meaning of the verse would be: "Intercessors will not intercede except for those who say: There is no god but Allah," that is, the believers, like what we find where the Qur'an says:

﴿ وَلا يَشْفَعُونَ إِلاَّ لِمَنِ ارْتَضَى ﴾

[150] Sūrat Maryam [Mary],19:87.

*They only intercede for one who is accepted.*[151]

However, the resulting meaning: they do not possess intercession for anyone except those who made a covenant etc. is far-fetched and somewhat constrained.

The best commentary of Allah's statement "They do not possess" is "They do not obtain." Then, the expression of the exception "save those who..." is admissible without implying something in addition, and the meaning is asserted: "He does not possess intercession except the one who says: There is no god but Allah." That is, only the believers intercede. This is like the verse:

﴿وَلا يَمْلِكُ الَّذِينَ يَدْعُونَ مِن دُونِهِ الشَّفَاعَةَ إِلاَّ مَن شَهِدَ بِالْحَقِّ وَهُمْ يَعْلَمُونَ﴾

*And those unto whom they call instead of Him possess no power of intercession except him who bears witness to the Truth.*[152]

The bearing witness to the Truth is the phrase: "There is no god but Allah."

Since what is meant by imploring Allah with the prophets, the saints, and the pious and by asking them for help is a request for their intercession, and since Allah has related that they possess intercession, then who can prevent anyone from seeking by permission of Allah what they possess by permission of Allah? Thus, it is permissible to ask from them that they give you what Allah has given to them. The only thing forbidden is asking intercession from idols which do not possess anything at all.

Another evidence is narrated by Ibn Majah with a sound chain of transmission on the authority of Abū Sa'id al-Khudri, may Allah be pleased with him. He relates that the Messenger of Allah said: "The one who leaves his house for prayer and then says: 'O Allah, I ask You by the right of those who ask You and I beseech

---

[151] Sūrat al-Anbiyā' [The Prophets], 21:28.
[152] Sūrat al-Zukhruf [Ornaments of Gold], 43:86.

You by the right of those who walk this path unto You, as my going forth bespeak not of levity, pride nor vainglory, nor is done for the sake of repute. I have gone forth solely in the warding off Your anger and for the seeking of Your pleasure. I ask You, therefore, to grant me refuge from hell fire and to forgive me my sins. For no one forgive sins but Yourself.' Allah will look kindly upon him and seventy thousand angels will seek his forgiveness."[153]

In this manner did the Prophet ﷺ make *tawassul* when he said "I ask You by the right of those who ask You," that is, by every believing servant. Moreover, he commanded his Companions to use this prayer when they made *duʿā* and to make *tawassul* just as he made *tawassul*. The Pious Ancestors (*al-Salaf*) of our faith among the Companions' Successors and their Successors continued to use this prayer upon their going out to prayer and no one disavowed them for it.

Among further evidences for the permissibility of *tawassul* is the occasion when the Prophet ﷺ said on the authority of Anas ibn Mālik: "O Allah, grant forgiveness to my mother, Fāṭima bint Asad, and make vast for her the place of her going in[154] by right of thy Prophet and that of those prophets who came before me" and so on until the end of the hadith. al-Ṭabarānī relates it in al-Kabīr. Ibn Ḥibbān and al-Ḥākim declare it sound. The "Fāṭima" referred to here is the mother of Sayyidina ʿAlī who raised the Prophet ﷺ. Ibn Abī Shayba on the authority of Jābir relates a similar narrative. Similar also is what Ibn ʿAbd Al-Barr on the authority of Ibn ʿAbbās and Abū Nuʿaym in his *Hilya* on the

---

[153]Related in *Musnad Aḥmad* (3:21), Ibn Mājah (Masājid), al-Mundhirī in *al-Targhīb* (1:179), Ibn Khuzayma in his *Ṣaḥīḥ*, Ibn al-Sunnī, and Abū Nuʿaym. al-Ghazālī mentions it in the *Iḥyā'*, and al-ʿIrāqī said: it is *ḥasan*. Al-Nawawī mentions Ibn al-Sunnī's two chains in the *al-Adhkār* and says they are weak. However, Ibn Ḥajar al-ʿAsqalānī says it is *ḥasan* in *al-Amālī al-Miṣriyyah* (#54) and in the *takhrīj* of Nawawī's book, explaining that the latter neglected Abū Saʿīd al-Khuḍrī's narration and omitted to mention Ibn Mājah's.

[154]I.e. her grave.

authority of Anas Ibn Malik relate, as al-Ḥāfiẓ al-Suyūṭī mentioned in the *Jami' al-Kabīr*.[155]

Also found as evidence: al-Tirmidhī, al-Nasā'ī, al-Bayhaqī, and al-Ṭabarānī relate with a sound chain that a blind man came to the Prophet ﷺ and said: "Pray to Allah that He relieve me." The Prophet ﷺ said: "If you wish I will pray, and if you wish you may be patient, and that is better." Then he prayed for him and commanded him to make ablution and do his ablution well and utter this prayer: "O Allah, I ask you and I address You by Your Prophet Muḥammad, the Prophet ﷺ of Mercy. O Muḥammad, I address by you my Lord in my need. O Allah, accept his intercession on my behalf." Then he returned and gained his sight. Al-Bukhārī produces this hadith in his *Tārīkh* (Biographical History), Ibn Mājah, and al-Ḥākim in *al-Mustadrak* with a sound chain of transmission. Suyūṭī in *al-Jami' al-Kabīr* and *al-Ṣaghīr* mentioned it also. It is therefore established that the Prophet ﷺ commanded the blind man to invoke him and implore Allah by means of him to accomplish his need.

The Wahhābis may claim that this is only in the life of the Prophet ﷺ and that it does not provide evidence for the permissibility of imploring Allah by means of him after death. We answer that this prayer has been used by the Companions and the Successors also after the repose of the Prophet ﷺ to accomplish their needs. The evidence for this is what al-Ṭabarānī and al-Bayhaqī have related, namely, that a man visited 'Uthmān ibn 'Affān, may Allah be pleased with him, during the time when he was Caliph, concerning a certain need he had but the noble Commander of the Faithful did not look immediately into it. The man complained to 'Uthmān ibn Ḥunayf who said to him: "Go and make ablution, then go to the mosque and pray in the

---

[155]Haythamī says in *Majma' al-Zawā'id*: "Ṭabarānī's chain contains Rawḥ ibn Ṣalāḥ who has some weakness but Ibn Ḥibbān and al-Ḥākim declared him trustworthy. The rest of its sub-narrators are the men of sound hadith."

following manner: "O Allah, I ask you and address you by your Prophet Muḥammad, the Prophet of Mercy. O Muḥammad, I address my Lord by you to accomplish my need." Then mention your need." So the man went away and did precisely as he was told and came back to the door of 'Uthmān ibn 'Affān. Then the doorkeeper came to him, took his hand, brought him into the presence of 'Uthman and made him to sit down with him. 'Uthman said: "Tell me what you need" and he mentioned his need and it was fulfilled. Then the Caliph said to him: "Whatever need you have, mention it to me." When the man went out of his presence he met Ibn Hunayf and said: "May Allah reward you with good for he would have not looked into my need until you spoke to him for me." But Ibn Hunayf said: "By Allah I did not speak to him, but I witnessed Allah's Messenger when the blind man came to him and complained about losing his sight."[156]

Such an act constitutes *tawassul* and he called upon him after the death of the Prophet ﷺ on the grounds that the Prophet ﷺ is living in his grave and his rank is above the rank of the Martyrs whom Allah has expressly said that they are living, being provided for, with their Lord.

Another evidence for *tawassul* is what al-Bayhaqī and Ibn Abi Shayba relate with a sound chain of transmission that a drought afflicted the people during the caliphate of 'Umar, may Allah be pleased with him, and Bilāl Ibn al-Harith came to the grave of the Prophet ﷺ and said: "O Messenger of Allah, ask for rain for your community, for they are being destroyed." Then the Messenger of Allah came to him in a dream and said to him that they would have water. This evidence of ours is not in the vision of the Prophet ﷺ. Even if his vision is true, the legal rulings of the Shari'a are not established by dreams, where there is room to cast

[156]Sound (*ṣaḥīḥ*) hadith related by Bayhaqī, Abū Nu'aym in the *Ma'rifa*, Mundhiri (*Targhīb* 1:473-474), Haythamī, and Ṭabarānī in the *Kabīr* (9:17-18) and the *Ṣaghīr* (1:184/201-202) on the authority of 'Uthmān ibn Ḥunayf's nephew Abū Imām a ibn Sahl ibn Ḥunayf.

doubt on the words or perspicuity of the dreamer. The evidence we are citing lies in the action of one of the Companions while that Companion was awake. That is Bilāl ibn al-Ḥārith who came to the grave of the Prophet ﷺ and called on him and made a request of him to provide his community with rain.[157]

Again, we find evidence in the *Ṣaḥīḥ* of Bukhārī from a narration of Anas Ibn Mālik from ʿUmar Ibn al-Khaṭṭāb in the time when he was Caliph asking for rain by means of al-ʿAbbās, the uncle of the Prophet ﷺ, when there was a drought in the Year of "Ramaḍa" (the Year of Destruction in 17 A.H.), then they received rain. And in *al-Mawāhib al-laduniyya* of the savant al-Qastallani we find that when ʿUmar asked through al-ʿAbbās for rain, he said: "O people, the Messenger of Allah used to see in al-ʿAbbas what a son sees in a father," whereupon they followed the Prophet's model in his behavior with al-ʿAbbās and took the latter as a means to Allah.

There is no difference in the *tawassul* or imploring by naming prophets and other pious persons and them being alive or dead because in neither state do they differ in anything whatsoever. In either state, producing an effect on states of affairs is not up to them. Creation, bringing into existence, producing an effect on states of affairs: all of this belongs to Allah alone, who has no partner in this or anything else. As for the one who believes that producing effects belongs only to the living, it is up to them to

---

[157]Ibn Kathīr cites it from Bayhaqī in *al-Bidāya wa al-Nihāya* (7:92) and says: *isnaduhu ṣaḥīḥ*; Ibn Abī Shayba cites it in his *Muṣannaf* with a sound (*ṣaḥīḥ*) chain as confirmed by Ibn Ḥajar who says: *rawā Ibn Abī Shayba bi isnādin ṣaḥīḥ* and cites the hadith in *Fatḥ al-Bārī, Istisqā'*, chap. 3 (Beirut: Dār al-kutub al-ʿilmiyya, 1410/1989 2:629-630). Ibn Ḥajar says that the man who visited and saw the Prophet ﷺ in his dream is identified as the Companion Bilāl ibn al-Ḥārith. He counts this hadith as one of the reason for Bukhārī's naming of the chapter "The people's request to their leader for rain if they suffer drought."
In his edition of Ibn Ḥajar, the Wahhābī scholar Ibn Bāz rejects the hadith as a valid source for seeking rain through the Prophet ﷺ—although it is established that the hadith is *ṣaḥīḥ*—and condemns the act of the ṣaḥābī who came to the grave, calling it "*munkar*" and "*wasīlatan ilā al-shirk.*" *Fatḥ al-Bārī* 2:630n.

differentiate between imploring Allah for the sake of the living or imploring Allah for the sake of the dead. For our part we say that Allah is the Creator of all things regardless, and:

﴿وَٱللَّهُ خَلَقَكُمْ وَمَا تَعْمَلُونَ﴾

*Allah has created you and all you do.*[158]

The Wahhābis who make a great show of their defense of monotheism and permit using only living persons as a means have made themselves fall into the sin of associating a partner with Allah (*shirk*) insofar as they believe, in their ignorance, that living beings have an effect upon things when in reality no one produces an effect except Allah.

Using as means (*tawassul*), or using as intermediary (*tashaffuʿ*), or asking for help (*istighātha*) a single person: the upshot of all this is the same, the aim of it being only to get blessings (*tabarruk*) by mentioning the names of beloved servants of Allah for whose sake Allah may grant mercy to creation, be they living or dead. The actual author of existence is Allah alone, they are only customary causes (*asbāb ʿādiyya*), they produce no effect on their own.

## Their Condemnation of *Nidā'* (Calling Out) and Seeking Madad

As for the invocations of common Muslim people in Arabic like: "O ʿAbd al-Qādir Gilānī look at me (*Yā ʿAbd al-Qādir, adriknī*)!" and "O Aḥmad al-Badawī give us support (*Yā Badawī madad*)!" they belong to the figurative language of the mind just as the application of someone who says to his food: "Satisfy me!" or to his water: "Quench my thirst!" or to his medicine: "Heal me!" The food does not satisfy, nor does the water quench the thirst, nor the medicine heal. But the One who is the real Satisfier of our hunger, the Quencher of our thirst and the Healer

[158] Sūrat al-Ṣāffāt [The Rangers], 37:96.

of our ills is Allah alone. The food, the water, the medicine are only the proximate or secondary causes which custom has established on the surface of things by our mind's regular association of them with certain concomitant events.

The majority of the Muslim community agree on the permissibility of imploring Allah for the sake of the Prophet ﷺ, the Companions, and the pious. From many of the Companions, the *'Ulamā'* of the Pious Ancestors, and those in succeeding generations, the meeting together of a majority on what is forbidden and idolatrous is not allowable because of the Prophet's sound hadith which some consider *mutawātir*:[159] "My community will not come together on an error"[160] and because Allah said:

﴿كُنتُمْ خَيْرَ أُمَّةٍ أُخْرِجَتْ لِلنَّاسِ﴾

*You are the best community of mankind which has been produced;*[161]

then how could all of them or the majority of them come together on what is erroneous?

One of the evidences permitting the seeking of help is what Bukhārī has related in a sound hadith from Ibn 'Abbās that the Prophet ﷺ mentioned in the story of Ḥajar, the mother of Isma'il: when thirst overtook her and her son, she began to run in search for water, then she heard a voice yet saw no one and she said: "If there be help (*ghawth*) with you, then help us (*aghith*)."[162] If seeking aid of other than Allah was *shirk* then why did she seek aid? Why did the Prophet ﷺ mention it to his Companions and not reject it? And why did the Companions after him transmit it and the narrators of hadith mention it?

---

[159] I.e. of definite authenticity and commanding belief.
[160] Already referenced in the section on *ijma'*.
[161] Sūrat Āli-'Imrān [The Family of Āli-'Imrān], 3:110)
[162] *Ṣaḥīḥ al-Bukhārī*, Kitab al-anbiyā'.

Bukhārī also relates in the Hadith of Intercession[163] that people, while they are in the horrors in the Day of Resurrection, ask help of Adam, then of Noah, then of Abraham, then of Moses, then of Jesus, and all of them will give an excuse, and Jesus will say: "Go to Muḥammad." Then they will go to Muḥammad and then he will say: "I will do it." If seeking aid of a creature was forbidden then the Prophet ﷺ would have not mentioned to the Companions. The ones who object to this give the answer that this is the Day of Resurrection when the Prophet ﷺ has power. One responds with the refutation that in their worldly life they have no power except as a secondary cause: likewise after death, the living in their graves and beyond are allowed to be secondary causes only.

Al-Ṭabarānī has related from 'Utbah ibn Ghazwān from the Prophet ﷺ that he said: "If one of you loses his way with respect to anything whatsoever or wishes help when he is in a land in which he has no friend let him say: O servants of Allah help me (*yā 'ibād Allāh a'īnūnī*)! for Allah has servants whom he does not see."[164]

---

[163]*Kitab al-tawḥīd.*

[164]*Ḥadīth ḥasan* (fair) related by Ṭabarānī in *al-Kabīr*, Abū Ya'lā, Ibn al-Sunnī, and Haythamī in *Majma' al-Zawā'id* 10:132. Bayhaqī relates something close to it on the authority of Ibn 'Abbās in *Kitāb al-Ādāb* (p. 436):"Allah has angels on earth who keep a record even of the leaves that fall on the ground. Therefore, f one of you has a lameness in his leg or finds himself in need in a deserted place of the earth, let him say: *a'īnū 'ibād Allāh raḥimakum Allāh* 'Help, O servants of Allah, may Allah have mercy on you!' Verily, he shall be helped, if Allah wills."

Ibn Ḥajar said its chain is fair (*isnāduhu ḥasan*) in *al-Amālī*. Bayhaqī relates it with two more chains from Ibn 'Abbās in *Shu'ab al-Īmān* (1:183 #167; 6:128 #7697), and another from Ibn Mas'ūd in *Ḥayāt al-Anbiyā' ba'da wafātihim* (p. 44), also related in *al-Kabīr* by Ṭabarānī, who has *yā 'ibād Allāh a'īnū* repeated three times, Ibn al-Sunnī, Abū Ya'lā, and Nawawī in *al-Adhkār*. Ibn Abī Shaybah relates in his *Muṣannaf* (7:103) through Abān ibn Ṣāliḥ that the Prophet ﷺ said:

"If one of you loses his animal or his camel in a deserted land where there is no one in sight, let him say: *yā 'ibād Allāh a'īnūnī*, 'O servants of Allah, help me!'Verily, he will be helped."

It is not said that all that is meant by the "servants of Allah" in the hadith cited above are only angels, or Muslims among the jinn, or men of the realm of the invisible: for all of these are living.[165] Hence, the hadith would not give evidence for asking aid from the dead, but this is not the case. We mention this because there is nothing explicit in the hadith whereby what is meant by "servants of Allah" are the categories we mentioned above and nothing else. Yet even if we were to concede this, the hadith would still be a proof against the Wahhābis from another standpoint, and that is the calling on someone invisible. The Wahhābis no more allow it than the calling on the dead.[166]

Furthermore, their contestation for some of the narrators of this hadith is pointless. It was narrated through a variety of paths of transmission, one of which supports the other. Thus, al-Ḥākim related it in his book of sound hadith as well as Abū 'Uwāna[167] and al-Bazzār with a sound chain of transmission from the Prophet ﷺ in this form: "If the mount of one of you runs loose in a desert land, let him call: O servants of Allah, restrain my beast! (*Yā 'ibād Allāh, aḥbisū*)." Shaykh al-Islam Ibn Taymiyya has mentioned this hadith in his book *al-Kalim al-Ṭayyib*, also Ibn Qayyim in his own *al-Kalim al-Ṭayyib*, Nawawī in his *Adhkār*, al-Jazarī in *Al-Ḥiṣn al-Ḥaṣīn*, and other transmitters of hadith whose number is too large to count. The latter wording is from the narrative of Ibn Mas'ud ؓ whose chain of transmission is continuous back to the Prophet ﷺ. The narration of Ibn Mas'ūd

---

The latter is the same as Bayhaqī's narration #167 from Ibn 'Abbās.

[165]I.e. there is no controversy about asking their help.

[166]Shawkānī allows the calling on someone invisible: "In the hadith (of *a'inu*) there is evidence that it is permissible to ask help from those one does not see among the servants of Allah, whether angels or good jinn, and there is nothing wrong in doing it, just as it is permissible for someone to seek the help of human beings if his mount becomes unmanageable or runs loose." *Tuḥfat al-Dhākirīn* p. 155-156.

[167] Abū 'Uwāna Ya'qūb ibn Isḥāq al-Isfarāyinī (337 AH/948CE - 418 AH/1027CE), a compiler of hadith whose work notably includes a *Musnad* arranged by *isnād* and subject.

whose chain is interrupted is: "Let him call: O servants of Allah, help me (*A'īnūnī yā 'ibād Allāh*)."[168]

There is also transmitted on the authority of 'Abd Allāh Ibn al-Imam Aḥmad Ibn Ḥanbal that he said: "I heard my father say: "I had made Hajj five times and once I got lost on the way. I was walking and I began to say: O servants of Allah, show us the way! I continued to say this until I got on the right way."169

One of the Wahhābis' pretexts in declaring disbeliever anyone who asks for help or calls on an absent prophet or saint who has died is that the call of people who beseech help from an absent prophet or saint might be in numerous places at one and the same time, and the number of the callers exceedingly large, mounting to hundreds of thousands. Yet and still, they claim, the ones asking for help believe that the one who is called upon is present at that very moment—not to mention their view that it is disbelief and *shirk* because of attributing to the person called upon for help the characteristics of Allah, since they are impossible for the ordinary mind to conceive when attributed to a human being. For it is obvious that one body cannot be existent in numerous places at one time.

---

[168]Ibn Mas'ūd's narration of *ahbisu* is the weaker of the chains and 'Utba's narration of *a'īnū* the stronger. Ibn Ḥajar said of the former, as reported by Ibn 'Allān in his *Futuḥāt* (5:145): "A rare (*gharīb*) hadith related by Ibn al-Sunnī (#508) and Ṭabarānī (cf. Munawī in *Fayḍ al-Qadīr* 1:307) and its chain is interrupted." Both Ibn Ḥajar and al-Haythamī (*Majma'* 10:132) said: "Its chain contains Ma'rūf ibn Ḥasan who is weak." (Shawkānī mentions that Abū Ya'lā cites it also.) However, as the third previous note shows, the hadith *a'īnū* is established as authentic.

Nawawī relates in *Al-adhkār* after mentioning the hadith *aḥbisū*: "One of our very knowledgeable teachers related to me that one day his animal ran loose—I think it was a mule—and he knew that hadith, so he said it, and Allah restrained it for them on the spot. I myself was with a group one time when one of their animals broke free and they were unable to restrain it, so I said it: it stopped on the spot with no reason other than those words." Shawkānī cites Nawawī's two accounts in his *Tuḥfat al-Dhākirīn*.

[169]Reported by Ibn Mufliḥ al-Ḥanbalī in his book *al-Ādāb al-Shar'īya*.

The answer is that Muslims do not believe that the person called upon is present in person at the time he is called in a number of places. That counts as disbelief. Besides, omnipresence of this order is impossible. What the callers believe is that the *baraka*, that is, the blessing or grace of the one called, is present in those places in a subtle fashion by Allah's act of creation and motivated by His mercy for the person asking for help out of respect for the one whom he calls on. That is not impossible, for the mercy of Allah is wide and without limit.

Then, when the Wahhābis attribute to Muslims this belief (omnipresence in person) of which they are completely innocent, they apply to it the criterion of invalidity which the jurists apply in the conditions of marriage if, as they note, a man marries a woman "by witness of Allah *and* his Messenger": the marriage contract is invalid. The Wahhābis then claim: if the Prophet ﷺ knows of the call of someone who is asking for help when he calls out to him from afar, then he would be the Knower of the invisible and the contract of marriage which the jurists say is invalid would be sound.

The answer is that Muslims just as they do not believe the Prophet ﷺ or a saint asked for help is present when he is called; likewise they do not attribute knowledge of the invisible to anyone except Allah, the Exalted. As for the absence of the validity of a marriage contract by witness of Allah *and* His Messenger, it is because Islamic Law makes the eye-witness testimony a condition of marriage and acts like it to preserve the marriage rights; since disputes may arise between the partners to the marriage which may eventually come before judges. Then it will be impossible for one or the other of the disputing parties to establish his claim by the witness of Allah and His Messenger. For suppose that Allah—who transcends what the obscurantists say—is indeed a body who comes down to the lower heaven as the Wahhābis claim: then we would say it would be a common phenomenon for him to descend to the courtroom so that His testimony before it might be produced to decisively settle the dispute of the two contending parties!

You know that the Wahhābis declare one who calls on other than Allah a disbeliever; for example, one who says "O Messenger of Allah" (*Yā Rasūl Allāh*) and so forth. Yet if we go to look we see that this purported disbelief of one who says "O Messenger of Allah!" for example, implies two suppositions: either he believes that the individual whom he calls is himself present at the time of his call, hears his call, accomplishes his need because of it and saves him from the difficulty for which he called him in the first place; or he believes that the one whom he calls hears by Allah's hearing, purely through Allah's own power, and that Allah and no one else accomplished his need in virtue of the *baraka* of the one on whom he calls; and, moreover, that it is Allah who delivers him from the difficulty which he is in, for the honor of that Prophet.

Either supposition shows some fault of thinking on the part of the Wahhābi who claims that the caller is a disbeliever. As for the first, anyone who believes that someone else other than Allah accomplishes his need and saves him from difficulty is a disbeliever *whether he calls out or never calls out to anyone* and it is incorrect to make his disbelief depend on the circumstance of calling out. You know that no Muslim believes this doctrine. As for the second supposition, one whose heart is the seat of faith[170] and who believes that the one who accomplishes needs and saves from perils is Allah alone, not someone else: it is not allowed that such a person be called an unbeliever solely on the basis of calling out to someone absent while believing that Allah creates the hearing in him.

The Wahhābis have shown ignorance in saying, at this juncture of the argument, that Islamic Law judges on the basis of externals (*al-ḥukm bi al-ẓāhir*), and that the external sense of calling upon someone other than Allah is that the caller believes in that other as having all-encompassing knowledge of the unseen and possessing an effective power to accomplish needs

[170] I.e. a Muslim.

and complete disposal over the universe! Yet, they say, complete knowledge of the unseen and effective power to accomplish the needs of creatures are characteristics peculiar to the Creator: therefore, they conclude, belief that someone other than Allah is characterized in this way automatically constitutes ascribing a partner to Allah and disbelief.

The answer is that the external interpretation of the frame of mind of a person who supplicates someone other than Allah signifies only that the caller has called other than Allah. It does not signify that he believes that the one he calls has power to carry out one's needs nor any of the other attributes the Wahhābis mention.

Belief is an inward matter of which certain external phenomena might give indications. The act of calling is not one of them. Say to the Wahhābis who deem the external meaning of calling to be an indication of idolatry and disbelief: Why is it most of you don't consider what belongs to the Muslim whom you call a disbeliever from the side of his external behavior manifest in acts of prayer, fasting, zakat, and the other pillars of the Faith? Why do you not look at these as indicators of his faith and sound belief? What is more amazing, that same Muslim who engages in supplication, clearly articulates (by keeping the pillars) his disbelief in the power of the one he calls to and in anything that goes with it. Yet despite this, you use this single external act of his as an indicator of that very belief which he has denied of himself. Would that I knew by what legal rule you can prove from the external significance of a man's call (*nidā'*) that his belief is deviant in the face of all the clear indications he gives you that his belief is sound.[171]

---

[171]From Abū Hurayra: I heard the Prophet ﷺ say: "By the one in Whose hand is Abū al-Qasim's soul, 'Isā ibn Maryam shall descend as a just and wise ruler. He shall destroy the cross, slay the swine, eradicate discord and grudges, and money shall be offered to him but he will not accept it. Then he shall stand at my graveside and say: *Yā Muḥammad!* and I will answer him."

## 12: Wahhābis Claim: Anyone Visiting a Grave is a Disbeliever

Should one inquire as to the nature of Wahhābi doctrine and be curious as to what its objective is, the answer to both questions is easily summed up. It is their declaring all Muslims unbelievers. This answer is a sufficient definition of their entire school of thought. For the one who looks closely into the ideas they introduce will find that in each question that school strives to declare all Muslims unbelievers, even though Allah Himself is pleased with Islam as their religion:

- they have declared Muslims unbelievers for their assertion that Allah the Exalted transcends corporeality;

---

Abū Ya'lā relates it with a sound chain in his *Musnad* (Dār al-Ma'mūn, ed. 1407/1987) 11:462; Ibn Ḥajar cites it in *al-Maṭālib al-'Āliyah* (Kuwait, 1393/1973) 4:23, chapter entitled: "The Prophet's life in his grave" and #4574; Haythamī says in *Majma' al-Zawā'id* (8:5), chapter entitled: "'Īsā ibn Maryam's Descent": "Its sub-narrators are the men of sound (*ṣaḥīḥ*) hadith."

Bukhārī in his *Adab al-mufrad*, Nawawī in his *Adhkār*, and Shawkānī in *Tuḥfat al-Dhākirīn* all relate the narrations of Ibn 'Umar and Ibn 'Abbās whereby they would call out *Yā Muḥammad* whenever they had a cramp in their leg (Chapters entitled: *Mā yaqūlu idhā akhadathu al-kharṣ fī rijlih* "What one says if he feels a cramp in his leg"). Regardless of the grade of these narrations, it is significant that Bukhārī, Nawawī, and Shawkānī never raised such a disturbing notion as to say that calling out "O Muḥammad" amounted to *shirk*.

See the following editions:

Nawawī's *al-Adhkār*:

    1970 Riyadh edition: p. 271
    1988 Ta'if edition: p. 383
    1992 Mecca edition: p. 370

Bukhārī's *Adab al-mufrad*:

    1990 'Abd al-Baqi Beirut edition: p. 286
    1994 Albani edition entitled *Da'if al-adab al-mufrad*: p. 87
    The latter gives as a reference: *Takhrij al-kalim al-tayyib* (235)"
    date? Beirut: 'Alam al-kitab: p. 324
    date? Beirut: Dar al-kutub al-'ilmiyya: p.142.

Shawkānī's *Tuḥfat al-Dhākirīn*:

    1970 Beirut: Dar al-kutub al-'ilmiyya: p. 206-207.

- they have declared Muslims unbelievers for their acceptance of Consensus is unbelief;
- they have declared Muslims unbelievers for their unquestioning emulation (*taqlīd*) of the legal rulings concerning the faith made by the Imams, the *Mujtahid*s of the four schools of Islamic law;
- they have declared Muslims unbelievers for their seeking the Prophet's intercession (*istishfāʿ*) after his death and using him as a means to Allah (*tawassul*);
- they have declared Muslims unbelievers for their visitation of graves.

To anyone who has eyes to see, it is obvious that a visitor to a grave either aims at seeking intercession, using as means to Allah those buried there and seeking to be blessed by visiting them, as in the case of visitation of places where prophets and saints are buried; or, on the other hand, the purpose may be consideration of the departed folk in order to strengthen feelings of humility in the heart and attain reward by reading the opening chapter of the Qur'an and asking Allah to forgive them, as when one visits the graves of all Muslims. Or, yet again, the aim of visitation may be remembrance of relatives and the departed beloved and visiting those whom fate has snatched away, of early making their graves their abodes. He remembers that they left him never to return again, feeling grief at their leave, his mind's tongue moving to express itself in lines like the following:

*O thou departing hence in pomp and power,*
*Tarry a while, for thy ransom is pomp and power.*
*Do not make haste, but walk humbly,*
*For thou art leaving never to return again.*

His sensibilities impel him to visit their graves, pausing at the traces of their tombs to shed sad tears over their remains and express their sorrow in lines like the following:

*Gone are those dear to me!*
*and I remain, like a lone sword.*
*How many a brother dearly beloved*
*I laid in his grave by my own hand!*

There is not in any of these practices one thing which calls for labeling as an unbeliever a Muslim bearing witness that there is no god but Allah and Muḥammad is the Messenger of Allah. I do not think that even the uneducated and gullible among people, not to mention the learned person versed in Islamic Law, is ever so impelled by his ignorance as to intend, by his visitation of a grave, to worship it; nor that he would ever believe that the grave itself accomplishes his need and creates what he wants.

## The Prophet's ﷺ Order to Visit Graves

The Prophet ﷺ said: "I forbade you in the past to visit graves, but visit them. (For visiting graves promotes renunciation of this World and remembrance of the Hereafter)."[172] As for travels to visit graves, the *'Ulamā'* have had different opinions about it. Some of them make it illicit (*ḥarām*) giving as evidence the words of the Prophet ﷺ: "Do not travel except to three mosques: the Masjid al-Ḥarām, this Masjid here in Madina, and Masjid al-Aqsa (in Jerusalem)." This is related by Bukhārī, Muslim and al-Tirmidhī. Al-Qāḍī Ḥusayn al-Marwazī (d. 462H) and al-Qāḍī 'Iyāḍ (d. 544H) have opted to forbid travel for visitation to graves[173] while others have permitted it, among them Imam al-Haramayn al-Juwayni and others. The proof they adduce for its permissibility is the Prophet's ﷺ statement: "I have forbidden you in the past to visit graves, but visit them." They said the Prophet

[172]Muslim (Kitāb al-Janā'iz, penultimate chapter; Aḍāḥī 37); Abū Dāwūd (Kitāb al-Janā'iz 77; Ashriba 7); Tirmidhī (Jana'iz 7, 60); Nisa'i (Kitāb al-Janā'iz 100; Daḥāyā 39; Ashriba 40); Ibn Mājah (Jana'iz 47); Aḥmad (1:145, 452; 3:38, 63, 66, 237, 250; 5:350, 355-357, 359, 361).

[173]This prohibition does not include the grave of the Prophet ﷺ, concerning which the view of al-Qāḍī 'Iyāḍ (d. 544H) and al-Qāḍī Ḥusayn al-Marwazī (d. 462H) accords with the consensus (ijmā'), namely that its visitation is a *sunna mustaḥabba.*

ﷺ has commanded us in this hadith to visit graves, and that he did not differentiate between graves that are near and graves that are far and to visit which travel becomes necessary.

As for the hadith: "Do not travel except to three mosques..." he only forbade frequency of travel to mosques not to places of religious visitation, just as is clear from his words. He only forbade frequency of travel to mosques because one mosque is like the other and no city is devoid of a mosque; so there is no need for a journey. This is not the case with graves that are places of visitation. They are not equal in blessing just as the hierarchical standing of their inhabitants differs in the view of Allah.

Without doubt, the exception expressed: "...except for three mosques" has several ramifications. Its meaning may be either the remote genus as when one says: "Do not travel anywhere except to three mosques." According to this meaning it is prohibited to travel anywhere other than what is expressed in the exception: this means that travel is illicit even for jihad, trading and commerce, gaining livelihood, acquiring knowledge and for pleasure and so forth. This cannot be the case. As for the proximate genus the meaning is: do not undertake travel to any mosque except to three. This is the correct interpretation. The hadith is specific in forbidding travel to all mosques except three. Thus, it is evidence for the permissibility for travel to visit graves.

ʿUmar, may Allah be pleased with him, after the conquest of Damascus said to Kaʿb al-Aḥbār: "O Kaʿb, do you wish to come with us to Madina to visit the Messenger of Allah?" Kaʿb answered: "Yes, O Commander of the Faithful." Similarly, we have evidence of Bilāl's coming from Damascus to Madina to visit the grave of the Prophet ﷺ. This took place during the caliphate of ʿUmar.[174]

Among those who say that traveling to visit graves is permissible we find Imam al-Nawawī, al-Qasṭallānī, and Imām al-Ghazālī. The latter said in his *Iḥyāʾ ʿUlūm al-Dīn* after mentioning the hadith: "Do not travel...": "The gist of the matter is that some *ʿUlamāʾ* use it as evidence for prohibiting travel to places of religious visitation and pilgrimage. It is clear to me that this is not the case. On the contrary, visitation to graves is commanded by the hadith: "I have forbidden you in the past to visit graves, but visit them." The hadith only mentions the prohibition of visitation to other mosques than the three Mosques because of the likeness of one mosque to another. Furthermore, there is no city in which there is no mosque. Hence, there is no need to travel to another mosque. As for places of religious visitation, the *baraka* of visiting them varies to the measure of their rank with Allah."

Touching on the issue of whether dead people hear or not, our view is as follows. It is well known that hearing in living people is actually a property of spirit (*al-Rūḥ*). The ear is only an organ or rather instrument of hearing, nothing more. Since the spirit of the dead person does not become extinct with the extinction of his body, the belief that the spirit hears is not farfetched. One cannot claim that it does not hear due to loss of the organ of hearing by reason of the body's perishing. For we say that it sometimes hears even without that organ just as in visions. Thus, the spirit talks and hears in its sleep just as it sees in dreams without mediation of an instrument, that is, an organ of sensation. Then, is it too much for the rational person, after experiencing sound and sight in one's sleep by the sole means of the spirit and without the slightest participation of the organs of sound and

---

[174]Shawkānī in *Nāyl al-Awṭār* confirms that Bilāl undertook travel for the express purpose of visiting the Prophet ﷺ according to a report with a good chain in ḥāfiẓ Ibn ʿAsākir's *Tārīkh Dimashq*.

sight, to believe that after the spirit separates from the body it hears and sees even without the organs of sound and sight?

Yet and still, the Wahhābis do not extend their denial that the dead can hear to martyrs because Allah says:

﴿وَلَا تَحْسَبَنَّ الَّذِينَ قُتِلُوا۟ فِى سَبِيلِ اللَّهِ أَمْوَٰتًا بَلْ أَحْيَآءٌ عِندَ رَبِّهِمْ يُرْزَقُونَ﴾

*Do not consider those who are slain for Allah's sake dead, but they are alive receiving sustenance with their Lord.*[175]

There is no doubt that the rank of prophets is not beneath the rank of martyrs: they, like them, are alive with their Lord, receiving sustenance. It has been narrated that the Prophet ﷺ said: "I passed by Musa on the night of my Journey while he was praying in his grave."[176] And on the authority of Anas the Prophet ﷺ said: "Prophets are alive in their graves [praying]."[177] Abū Ya'lā al-Mawṣilī and al-Bazzār relate this. On the authority

[175] Sūrat Āli-'Imrān [The Family of Āli-'Imrān], 3:169.

[176] A sound (*ṣaḥīḥ*) tradition related on the authority of Anas and others by Muslim, Nasā'ī, Bayhaqī in the *Dalā'il al-Nubuwwah* and the *Ḥayāt al-Anbiyā'*, and Suyūṭī in *Anbā' al-Adhkiyā'* and *Sharḥ al-Ṣudūr*. Nawawī said in his commentary on this hadith: "The work of the next world is all dhikr and *du'ā*"' (*Sharḥ Ṣaḥīḥ Muslim* 1/73/267).

[177] A sound (ṣaḥīḥ) tradition is related on the authority of Anas ibn Mālik (r) by al-Bazzār in his *Musnad*, Abū Ya'lā in his *Musnad*, Ibn 'Adī in *al-Kāmil fī al-Ḍu'afā'*, Tammām al-Rāzī in *al-Fawā'id*, al-Bayhaqī in *Ḥayāt al-Anbiyā' fī Qubūrihim*, Abū Nu'aym in *Akhbār Aṣbahān*, Ibn 'Asākir in *Tārīkh Dimashq*, al-Haythamī in *Majma' al-Zawā'id* (8:211), al-Suyūṭī in *Anbā' al-Adhkiyā' bi-Ḥayāt al-Anbiyā'* (#5), and al-Albānī in *Silsilat al-Aḥādīth al-Ṣaḥīḥah* (#621). Al-Suyūṭī adds: "The life of the Prophet ﷺ, in his grave, and [also] that of the rest of the prophets, is known to us as definitive knowledge ('ilman qaṭ'iyyan)." Sakhāwī, the student of Ibn Ḥajar al-'Asqalānī, said: "As for us (Muslims), we believe and confirm that he ﷺ is alive and provided for in his grave" (*al-Qawl al-Badī'*, p. 161). Ibn al-Qayyim said in *Kitāb al-Rūḥ*, p. 58: "It is obligatory knowledge to know that his body ﷺ is in the earth tender and humid (i.e., as in life), and when the Companions asked him: 'How is our greeting presented to you after you have turned to dust?' he replied: 'Allah has defended the earth from consuming the flesh of Prophets,' and if his body were not in his grave, he would not have given this answer."

of Ibn ʿUmar the Prophet ﷺ said: "I saw Jesus, Moses, and Abraham, on them be peace." This is related by Bukhārī, Muslim and Imam Mālik in his *Muwaṭṭaʾ*. Abū Bakr Aḥmad ibn Ḥusayn al-Bayhaqī recorded in *Shuʿab al-Īmān* on the authority of Abū Hurayra that the Prophet ﷺ said: "Whoever sends blessings on me at my grave, I will hear him, and whoever sends blessings on me from afar, I am informed about it."[178] Therefore, if the premise *prophets are alive* is affirmed, then, one must also affirm the premise *prophets can hear*; for hearing is a concomitant property of life.

It is incorrect to invoke the fact that since the life of prophets and martyrs in the *barzakh* or "isthmus life" is different from the life of this world they cannot hear. Even if we grant that the two lives are each of a different kind, nevertheless affirming "They are alive" with *any* kind of life is sufficient to establish that they hear and that their *tawassul* and supplication for help follows as a matter of course.

Finally, the organ of hearing itself, in prophets, is not voided by death: for their bodies do not suffer the corruption of the grave as we know from the noble hadith: "Allah has forbidden the earth to consume the bodies of Prophets."[179] If we were to slacken the reins and say it is true that the bodies of prophets undergo corruption in their graves as the Wahhābis claim, having already

---

[178]Abū al-Shaykh cites the narration in *Kitāb al-Ṣalāt ʿalā al-Nabī* (see *Jalāʾ al-Afhām*, p. 22); Ibn Ḥajar comments in *Fatḥ al-Bārī* (6:379), "Abū al-Shaykh cites it with a good chain (*sanad jayyid*)." Al-Bayhaqī mentions it in *Ḥayāt al-Anbiyāʾ* and in *Shuʿab al-Īmān* (2:218, #1583).

[179]A sound (*ṣaḥīḥ*) tradition is related on the authority of Aws ibn Aws al-Thaqafī by Aḥmad in his *Musnad*, Ibn Abī Shaybah in the *Muṣannaf*, Abū Dāwūd in the *Sunan*, al-Nasāʾī in his *Sunan*, Ibn Mājah in his *Sunan*, al-Dāramī in his *Musnad*, Ibn Khuzaymah in his *Ṣaḥīḥ*, Ibn Ḥibbān in his *Ṣaḥīḥ*, al-Ḥākim in the *Mustadrak*, al-Ṭabarānī in his *al-Kabīr*, al-Bayhaqī in *Ḥayāt al-Anbiyāʾ*, al-Suyūṭī in *Anbāʾ al-Adhkīyāʾ*, and al-Nawawī in *al-Adhkār*. Al-Dhahabī confirms al-Ḥākim's grading. Another version cited by Ibn Mājah contains the addition: "And the Prophet of Allah ﷺ is alive and provided for (*fa nabiyyullāhi ḥayyun yurzaq*)." Al-Bayhaqī also cites it in *al-Sunan al-Kubrā*.

affirmed that *they are alive and receiving sustenance[180]*, then, this would simply count as affirmation that they hear even though they lack an organ for this purpose according to the view we expounded above.

We have abundant evidence in hadith which provide evidence that other than prophets and martyrs among the dead can hear. Cited by Bukhārī and Muslim and the narrators of the *Sunan* is the hadith transmitted on the authority of Ibn ʿUmar ؓ who said: "The Messenger of Allah spoke to the People (buried) in the Well saying: 'Have you found out that what your Lord had promised you is true?' then someone exclaimed: 'Are you calling out to the dead!' The Prophet ﷺ replied: 'You do not hear better than they do, except they do not respond.'" And in Bukhārī and Muslim we find the ḥadīth of Anas on the authority of Abū Ṭalḥa that the Prophet ﷺ called to them: "Yā Abā Jahl ibn Hishām! Yā Umayya ibn Khalaf! Yā ʿUtbah ibn Rabīʿah! Have you not found that what your Lord promised you is true? For I have found that what He promised me is true." ʿUmar said to him: "O Messenger of Allah, how do you address bodies devoid of spirit?" The Prophet ﷺ replied: "By Him in Whose Hand is my soul! You do not hear what I am saying to them more clearly than they do."

Similarly, it has been affirmed in Bukhārī and Muslim on the authority of Anas ؓ that the Prophet ﷺ said: "Surely, when the servant of Allah is placed in his grave and his companions turn away from it, he hears the thumps of their sandaled feet."[181]

Abū Nuʿaym al-Iṣbahānī has mentioned with his chain of transmission from ʿUbayd ibn Marzūq, who said: "A woman of Madīnah, named Umm Miḥjan, used to sweep the mosque. Then she died. The Prophet ﷺ was not informed of this event.

---

[180] Sūrat Āli-ʿImrān [The Family of Āli-ʿImrān], 3:169.
[181] See also the "Chapter on the Proofs Used to Establish the Knowledge that the Dead Hear in the Graves" in Ibn al-Qayyim's *al-Rūḥ*, as well as similar chapters in al-Suyūṭī's *Sharḥ al-Ṣudūr*, Ibn al-Kharrāṭ's *al-ʿĀqibah*, Ibn Rajab's *Aḥwāl al-Qubūr*, al-Subkī's *Shifāʾ al-Siqām*, and others.

Thereafter, he passed by her grave and asked: 'What is this?' Those present replied: 'Umm Miḥjan.' He said: 'The one who swept the mosque?' They answered: 'Yes.' Thereupon the people lined up and prayed for her. Then he addressed her: 'Which deed of yours did you find more favored?' They exclaimed: 'O Messenger of Allah, can she hear you?' He replied: 'You cannot hear more clearly than she does.' Then it is mentioned that she answered him: 'Sweeping the mosque.' The chain of transmission in this ḥadīth is interrupted (*munqaṭi'*). There are other narrations resembling it."[182]

It is narrated concerning 'A'isha, may Allah be pleased with her, when she heard the hadith about the dead hearing, she denied it and said: "How does the Prophet ﷺ say something like that when Allah has said: "*You cannot make those to hear who are in the graves*".[183] While her opinion does not affirm the hearing of the dead as Ibn Taymiyya notes in his Legal Opinions (*Fatāwā*) and in other places, we have no excuse for following it. For the question necessarily concerns a well-known matter of faith which no one has permission to deny. In fact 'A'isha has also narrated that the Prophet ﷺ said, as Ibn Rajab has noted in *Aḥwāl al-Qubūr*: "Surely they know now that what I said to them is true." This narration of hers supports those which say that the dead hear, for if it is possible for a dead man to know, surely it is possible for him also to hear. Therefore, to affirm that they do know is necessarily also to affirm that they hear.

As for the Qur'anic verses:

﴿وَمَآ أَنتَ بِمُسْمِعٍ مَّن فِى ٱلْقُبُورِ﴾

*You cannot make those who are in the graves hear*;[184]

---

[182] Ibn Ḥajar states in *al-Iṣābah* (8:187): "Mihjanah, also named Umm Mihjan—a black woman who used to sweep the mosque [in Madīnah]. She is mentioned in the books of sound (*ṣaḥīḥ*) ḥadīth, but without being named."

[183] Sūrat al-Fāṭir[The Originator], 35:22.

[184] *Ibid.*

and:

﴿ إِنَّكَ لَا تُسْمِعُ ٱلْمَوْتَىٰ ﴾

*You cannot make the dead hear...*[185] there is no evidence in them for the denial of hearing in the case of the dead in the absolute sense, it is only evidence for denying hearing for those who benefit thereof.[186] That is because what is meant by the phrase: "*Those in the graves*" in the first verse and by "*the dead*" in the second verse are the unbelievers, who are compared to the dead lying in their graves. Just as the dead do not hear with a beneficial kind of hearing—that is, with a hearing made complete by the mutual exchange of address between the hearer and the speaker—in the same way the unbelievers do not hear the warning signs that the Prophet ﷺ addresses to them in a way that benefits them by guiding them to faith in Allah.

What otherwise confirms the above is that unqualified hearing is also an established attribute of the unbelievers: they hear what the Prophet ﷺ said to them; but they derived no benefit from it. This is confirmed by Allah's saying:

﴿ وَلَوْ عَلِمَ اللَّهُ فِيهِمْ خَيْرًا لَّأَسْمَعَهُمْ وَلَوْ أَسْمَعَهُمْ لَتَوَلَّوْا وَّهُم مُّعْرِضُونَ ﴾

*If Allah had recognized in them any good, He would, indeed, have made them hear: if He made them hear* (*as it stands*), *they would turn away*;[187].

Hence, what is meant by "hear" when He says "*He would indeed have made them hear*" is a hearing which brings benefit to the

---

[185] Sūrat al-Naml (The Ant), 27:80.

[186] See Ibn al-Qayyim's section "That the Hearing of the Dead is Real" in *al-Rūḥ* (Madīnah ed., 1984), p. 59: "The actual meaning of these verses (35:22 and 27:80) is: You cannot make those hear whom Allah does not wish to hear, for you are only a warner. That is: Allah has only given you the ability to warn, for which He has made you responsible; not that of making those hear whom Allah does not wish to hear."

[187] Sūrat al-Anfāl [The Spoils of War],8:23.

hearer and when He says: "*If He made them hear* (*as it stands*)" He means hearing which carries no benefit. If this were otherwise, the sense of the passage would be corrupt inasmuch as the verse would, then, be a syllogism where the middle term (He makes them hear) is reiterated; the end result would be: "If Allah had recognized any good in them, they would have turned away." This conclusion is absurd and contradictory, as you can see, since it would entail that the turning back take place—which is evil—despite the fact that Allah recognized good in them. Allah's recognition would be, in that case, a misrecognition with respect to the true state of the unbelievers—Exalted is Allah high above such a possibility.

The above cited two verses point to a further meaning: that what is meant by the hearing negated in both cases is the hearing connected with the faculty of guidance just as the context of the two verses indicate. The meaning then is that you do not guide the unbelievers by yourself, O Muḥammad! because they are like dead men and that you cannot cause the dead to hear by yourself. The only agent causing them to hear is Allah as the Qur'an says:

﴿ إِنَّكَ لَا تَهْدِي مَنْ أَحْبَبْتَ وَلَٰكِنَّ اللَّهَ يَهْدِي مَن يَشَاءُ ﴾

*You do not guide whom you like but Allah guides whom he wishes.*[188]

One does not say: "Just as the one making the dead to hear in reality is Allah, likewise, the one making the living to hear is in reality none other than He." For Allah is the Creator of all actions whatsoever, just as the true doctrine on the matter teaches. What, then, is the motivation for illustrating Allah's agency with the hearing of the dead? What we say is this:

> The fact that Allah alone is the one making the dead to hear is a matter admitting of no ambiguity even for a blind man. As for His being the one causing the living to

[188] Sūrat al-Qaṣaṣ [The Stories] 28:56.

> hear in reality, it is not said like that.[189] This is because one might falsely suppose that the Agent causing hearing in the one spoken to is the actual speaker, on the grounds that the hearing of the one spoken to directly follows the external voice issuing from the mouth of the person who addresses him. Hence to exemplify Allah's agency with the hearing of the living is improper. To give an example requires that its content be unambiguously clear; this is not the case in the category of living persons as we have explained.[190]

Since the unbelievers were alive, to illustrate the fact that the Prophet ﷺ cannot make them hear by comparing them to the living whom the Prophet ﷺ cannot cause to hear comes close to fashioning a comparison between a thing and itself, as we find in that given by the poet who said:

> *Surrounded as we are with water,*
> *We sit like people encircled by water.*

The Wahhābis respond, with regard to the hadith of the People of the Well, that the hearing experienced by the dead on the occasion when the Prophet ﷺ questioned them was a miracle proper only to him. It does not count as evidence, they claim, that these dead were also capable of hearing the speech of someone else. The answer to this is that the miracle is not a miracle unless its manifestation is a phenomenon experienced by other persons like the speaking of pebbles. The Companions were hearing the voice of the pebbles glorifying Allah while they were being held in the palm of the Prophet's hand.[191] But it is impossible that the

---

[189] I.e. it is inappropriate to use such terms.

[190] Zahāwī's point is that Allah highlighted the power to make the dead hear in the Qur'an as an example of His agency, because in the case of the dead, His agency is more evident to the mind than in the case of the living, although He equally effects the hearing of both the living and the dead.

[191] Hadīth of Abū Dharr, related by al-Haythamī in *Majma' al-Zawā'id*, with a sound (*ṣaḥīḥ*) chain, under the chapter entitled 'Alāmāt al-Nubuwwah (Signs of

dead's hearing of the Prophet ﷺ speaking to them be a miracle since it was not manifest to anyone but himself. Furthermore, the hadith reporting that the dead hear the thumping of sandaled feet (Bukhārī and Muslim) contravenes such a phenomenon being a miracle in the case of the People of the Well. For it indicates that dead people also hear the talk of other people besides the Prophet ﷺ.

The Wahhābis further respond that the object intended when the Prophet ﷺ spoke to the dead was admonition of the living and not to cause an act of understanding on the part of the dead. The answer to this is that if the intended object of his speech was admonition of the living, why did 'Umar ask: "How do you speak to bodies devoid of spirit?" out of astonishment at his speaking to them? I do not believe that fatuousness has pushed the Wahhābis to the point of thinking that after almost three-quarters of a millennium they understand what the Prophet ﷺ meant better than his Companion, 'Umar. Besides, the answer the Prophet ﷺ gave by itself constitutes denial that what he aimed at was admonition because he replied: "You do not hear better than they." This answer is obviously not suitable as an admonition. On the contrary, it is a clear rejection of 'Umar's sense of farfetchedness in the Prophet's behavior and astonishment because of it.

The Wahhābis, finally, answer that the Prophet ﷺ only spoke to the dead out of personal conviction that they hear. Thereafter, they claim, the two verses of the Qur'an were revealed to correct his belief. The response to this is that it is unallowable that the Prophet ﷺ believed anything like that of his own accord. On the contrary, it came about necessarily in virtue of revelation and inspiration from his Lord. Allah said of him:

---

Prophethood): "The Prophet ﷺ took pebbles and they glorified Allah in his hand; he put them down and they became silent..."

﴿وَمَا يَنطِقُ عَنِ ٱلْهَوَىٰٓ﴾

"*He does not speak of his own desire*".[192] This is especially the case since he did not arrive at his knowledge of the matter by merely exercising his faculty of reason. Rather, it came about by way of revelation and inspiration as we have said.

One piece of evidence that indicates that Allah quickens the dead in their graves so that they hear is His statement retelling the avowal of those who said:

﴿قَالُوا۟ رَبَّنَآ أَمَتَّنَا ٱثْنَتَيْنِ وَأَحْيَيْتَنَا ٱثْنَتَيْنِ﴾

"*Our Lord, twice hast Thou put us to death and twice hast Thou quickened us*".[193]

For what is meant by the first putting to death is the putting to death before resting in the grave. What is meant in the case of the other is the putting to death after resting in the grave. If Allah did not give life in the graves a second time, it would be impossible to put to death a second time. The Wahhābis answer this by saying that the first putting to death is the state of nonexistence prior to creation and the second putting to death is after creation. In truth, this is amusing even for children because putting to death can take place only after the occurrence of life and there is no life prior to Allah's creation of life. As for their response that the first putting to death is the putting to death of people after their life in the world of atoms, it is weaker than the first answer. People in the world of atoms were no different than spirits which Allah created and asked:

﴿أَلَسْتُ بِرَبِّكُمْ قَالُوا۟ بَلَىٰ﴾

"*Am I not your Lord?*" *and they answered, saying:* "*Yes!*"[194]

---

[192] Sūrat al-Najm[The Star],53:3.
[193] Sūrat Ghāfir [the Forgiver], 40:11

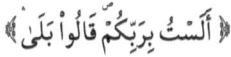

Moreover, the reader knows that death is defined as a separation of the soul from the body. Hence, there is no death prior to embodiment, although it is possible for Allah to annihilate spirits after creating them. But that has nothing to do with death as we have just defined it.

Finally, the Wahhābiyya usher forth evidence for the incapacity of dead people to hear on the basis of a legal ruling of the Shariʿa that *ʿUlamā ʾ* apply in the case where a man performs certain acts using such words as: "If I address X, my wife is divorced"—or: "my slave-girl is free." Now, if that man speaks to X after his death, then the divorce is invalid and the act of manumission null. They conclude that the basis of nullity and voidness is the fact that dead person lacks the faculty of hearing.

We refuse to grant that the basis of the ruling for the *ʿUlamā ʾ* is the absence of hearing on the part of the dead. On the contrary, they base themselves on what they know of custom, namely that it routinely makes the stipulating of oaths like the above, conditional on life. The whole benefit of speaking is the mutual exchange of communication, which does not place when one party of the communication is dead. Conversing with a dead person, therefore, does not qualify as speech only inasmuch as his death renders him powerless to respond—not because he is powerless to hear.

## 13: The Wahhābis' *Takfīr* of the One Who Swears, Makes a Vow, or Sacrifices by Other than Allah

May Allah the Exalted fight the Wahhābis because they are intent on establishing reasons to declare Muslims unbelievers. They have shown that *takfīr* is their highest ambition. You see them declaring as disbelievers persons who implore Allah for the sake of the Prophet ﷺ and seek his help by intercession to Allah to accomplish their needs, while not feeling the slightest shame

---

[194]Sūrat al-Aʿrāf [The Heights], 7:172.

in seeking help from unbelievers of the foreign states of Europe[195] in order to carry out their plans which are to subject the Muslims to their control, make war against them, and, in rebellion from the authority of the Commander of the Faithful, renounce allegiance to him and the obedience to him which Allah has ordered in the Qur'an as we have explained earlier. They have taken the enemies of Islam as intimate friends, asking them to aid them with military support in their corrupt purpose and using that support to perpetrate their stubborn harassment and error. Yet Allah has said:

﴿ يَا أَيُّهَا الَّذِينَ آمَنُواْ لاَ تَتَّخِذُواْ الْيَهُودَ وَالنَّصَارَى أَوْلِيَاء ﴾

*O ye who believe! take not the Jews and the Christians for your friends and protectors.*[196]

May our Lord remove the Wahhābis from the face of the earth. Do they not know that those same "friends" they make in order to subjugate Muslims to their tyranny, will, once they have gotten a foothold, in turn, subjugate and oppress them as well along with whomever else they consider adverse and opposed to their plans?

We have shown that the practice of the Wahhābis is to declare all Muslims disbelievers. As we already said, they claim they are unbelievers because they implore Allah for the sake of prophets and saints and, in addition, call on them for help. Wahhābis also claim that Muslims are unbelievers if they swear by the name of someone else than Allah and make vows to other than Him and sacrifice animals for their sake.

For the sake of argument, let us grant that certain doctrines which the Wahhābis attribute to Muslims are held by them and do in fact constitute disbelief, and that it is correct to say that the person asserting them has acted contrary to Islam. Even then, it

---

[195] And now America.

[196] Sūrat al-Mā'idah [The Table Spread], 5:51.

would still not be correct to pronounce the entire community of Muslims guilty of unbelief or even a specific Muslim individual. For the latter might have made such a statement lacking knowledge of whatever texts would obligate acknowledgment of the truth. Or it might be the case that such knowledge has not been suitably established in his view. Or perhaps he has not understood it and had what confuses him laid out in a fashion that allows him to beg forgiveness before Allah and seek proper excuses for his error. For the one who believes in Allah and His Messenger, Allah is a Forgiver of sins whether committed in thought, word, or deed. As for the more severe aspect of what He has revealed in the Qur'an concerning those who perpetrates those sins, it comes in the form of threats and, as it says, is meant for:

﴿ وَمَن يَقْتُلْ مُؤْمِنًا مُّتَعَمِّدًا فَجَزَاؤُهُ جَهَنَّمُ خَالِدًا فِيهَا ﴾

*Whoever kills a believer intentionally, his recompense is Hell to abide therein;*[197]

and:

﴿ إِنَّ الَّذِينَ يَأْكُلُونَ أَمْوَالَ الْيَتَامَى ظُلْمًا إِنَّمَا يَأْكُلُونَ فِى بُطُونِهِمْ نَارًا وَسَيَصْلَوْنَ سَعِيرًا ﴾

*Those who unjustly eat up the property of orphans, eat a fire into their own bodies: they will soon be enduring a blazing fire*[198]

and:

﴿ وَمَن يَعْصِ اللَّهَ وَرَسُولَهُ وَيَتَعَدَّ حُدُودَهُ يُدْخِلْهُ نَارًا خَالِدًا فِيهَا وَلَهُ عَذَابٌ مُّهِينٌ ﴾

*Those who disobey Allah and His Messenger and transgress His limits will be admitted to a Fire, to abide therein: and they shall have a humiliating punishment.*[199]

---

[197] Sūratu 'n-Nisā [Women], 4:93.
[198] Sūratu 'n-Nisā [Women], 4:10.
[199] Sūratu 'n-Nisā [Women], 4:14.

In his book *Madārij al-sālikīn*, Ibn al-Qayyim has made the statement, the gist of which is as follows: The adherents of the Sunna of the Prophet ﷺ are in complete agreement that Allah's friendship and enmity might be found in the single individual in two different respects: there might exist in him faith and hypocrisy, as well as faith and unbelief together. In addition, he will be close to Allah in one respect more than the other. Hence, of the people in one respect the Qur'an says:

﴿هُمْ لِلْكُفْرِ يَوْمَئِذٍ أَقْرَبُ مِنْهُمْ لِلإِيمَانِ﴾

*They were that day nearer to unbelief than to faith.*[200]

Associating a partner with Allah—*shirk*—falls into two classes: hidden and manifest. Hidden *shirk* might be forgiven. As for manifest *shirk*, there is no forgiveness for it without express repentance.

Now swearing by someone other than Allah—Ibn Qayyim continues—does not remove the one who does it from Islam, even though there is mentioned in a hadith narrated on the authority of Ibn ʿUmar that: "Whoever swears by someone other than Allah has associated a partner with Him."[201] And in another narration of the same hadith: "Whoever swears by someone other than Allah has committed an act of *kufr*." The leading scholars of hadith in the schools of Shafiʿi, Hanafi, Maliki and Hanbali law all construe *kufr* here to mean *kufr al-niʿma* or the failure to acknowledge Allah's favor or blessing. As for the *shirk* mentioned in the first narration, they find it to be *al-shirk al-khafī* or the kind that is hidden rather than manifest such as occurs when one performs an act of piety in order to show off. That does not remove a person from Islam. Yet it defeats the religious purpose of that act. On this much the *ʿUlamā*ʾ have reached a

---

[200] Sūrat Āli-ʿImrān [The Family of Āli-ʿImrān], 3:167.
[201] A sound (*ṣaḥīḥ*) hadith related by Abū Dāwūd, Iman 3:570 (3251), and Tirmidhī, Iman 5:253 (1535).

consensus so that those who follow the school of Imām al-Shāfi'ī, for example, says that it falls into the category of what is *makrūh tanzīhan*—reprehensible for purposes of scrupulous observance—rather than *makrūh taḥrīman*, or reprehensible to the point of prohibition and reprobation. Therefore, the mode of swearing about which the *'Ulamā'* disagree over whether it is reprehensible or prohibited cannot be said to make its perpetrator an unbeliever and thus remove him from Islam.[202]

As for the vow to someone other than Allah, both Shaykh Taqī al-Dīn Ibn Taymiyya and Ibn al-Qayyim—who are among the most critical concerning this question—said that it is not permissible and that it constitutes an act of disobedience. Neither said that it constitutes an act of unbelief or of *shirk* such as would remove one from Islam. Their position is that fulfilling such a vow is not allowable, but that if the vow is to give alms to some deserving person among the poor, then, it is good for him in the sight of Allah. Now, if the one making the vow to someone other than Allah were an unbeliever then they would not have ordered him to perform an act of charity since charity is unacceptable from an unbeliever. Rather, they would have ordered him to renew his Islam.

---

[202]This is Ibn Qayyim's text in Kitab al-Salat of the *Madārij*: "About Greater *Shirk* Allah says: '*Surely whoever ascribes partners to Allah, for him Allah has forbidden the Garden. His abode is the Fire. For wrong-doers there will be no helpers*' (5:72); and also: '*Whoever ascribes partners to Allah, it is as if he had fallen from the sky and the birds had snatched him or the wind blown him to a far-off place*' (22:31). About showing off He says: '*And whoever hopes for the meeting with his Lord, let him do righteous works, and associate no partner in the worship due only to his Lord*' (18:110)."

"On this same subject of Lesser *Shirk*, the Prophet ﷺ said: "Whoever swears an oath by other than Allah has associated something with Him." This was related by Abū Dāwūd and others. However, it is well known that swearing an oath by something other than Allah does not take one out of the community of the Muslims, and it does not make someone a disbeliever. In the same vein the Prophet ﷺ said: "*Shirk* in this Umma is stealthier than creeping ants." [Aḥmad 4:403; Albani considers it sound in *Ṣaḥīḥ al-Jami' al-ṣaghīr*, 3:333 (3624).]

As for the sacrifice for the sake of someone other than Allah, Ibn Qayyim categorizes it under things prohibited, not under act of unbelief, except when one sacrifices to something worshipped besides the Creator. Similarly, those versed in knowledge record that it is prohibited because it is for the sake of someone other than Allah. Nevertheless, they do not declare the one who performs such a sacrifice an unbeliever.

## Conclusion

What I intended to elaborate in this hastily thrown together work has now been accomplished. My purpose has been to prevent the spread of the Wahhābi school into Iraq and neighboring areas, to clarify for the individual reader the truth, and unveil for him what is correct. He should no longer be deceived by whatever this subversive sect publishes to infect with its views the ignorant and the simple-minded.

My efforts in this work have been aided by my brother and friend in Islam, the learned M'arūf Effendī al-Risāfī, may the Creator long sustain him. And praise belongs to Allah first and last.

The indigent one relying on Allah the Exalted
Jamīl Effendī Zahāwī Zādah
Beginning of Ramadan 1322 A.H. (1904 C.E.)

www.ingramcontent.com/pod-product-compliance
Lightning Source LLC
Chambersburg PA
CBHW030524080526
44586CB00011B/310
*9781938058738*